Faith to Foster

Faith to Foster

An All-American Story
of Loving the Least of These

T.J. and Jenn Menn

NASHVILLE

NEW YORK • MELBOURNE • VANCOUVER

Faith to Foster
An All-American Story of Loving the Least of These

Published in New York, New York, by Morgan James Publishing. Morgan James is a trademark of Morgan James, LLC. www.MorganJamesPublishing.com

The Morgan James Speakers Group can bring authors to your live event. For more information or to book an event visit The Morgan James Speakers Group at www.TheMorganJamesSpeakersGroup.com.

All scripture quotations, unless otherwise indicated, are taken from the Holy Bible, New International Version®, NIV®. Copyright ©1973, 1978, 1984, 2011 by Biblica, Inc.TM Used by permission of Zondervan. All rights reserved worldwide. www.zondervan.com The "NIV" and "New International Version" are trademarks registered in the United States Patent and Trademark Office by Biblica, Inc.TM

This book is a work of non-fiction, with names and identifying details changed to maintain confidentiality.

ISBN 978-1-68350-512-9 paperback
ISBN 978-1-68350-275-3 eBook
Library of Congress Control Number: 2017904942

Graphics credit: Used with permissions:
Figures from www.Decalopolis.com

Editing credit to Sandra Judd and Amy Boeke

Cover Design by:
Rachel Lopez
www.r2cdesign.com

Interior Design by:
Bonnie Bushman
The Whole Caboodle Graphic Design

In an effort to support local communities, raise awareness and funds, Morgan James Publishing donates a percentage of all book sales for the life of each book to Habitat for Humanity Peninsula and Greater Williamsburg.

Get involved today! Visit
www.MorganJamesBuilds.com

Table of Contents

Introduction

"Be on your guard. Stand firm in the faith. Be men of courage. Be strong. Do everything in love."
— The Apostle Paul, 1 Corinthians 16:13-14

Thank you for allowing us to share our story of foster parenting with you. Our faith motivated and sustained us, so we include it in our story, though some readers may find a few faith-related comments foreign. We believe a faith in Jesus Christ is a source of selfless love. Without Christ, we doubt we would have spent the time and energy parenting kids we knew would leave. We know it's going to hurt to love and attach to someone only to have the relationship torn away. But, in response to Jesus Christ's sacrificial love for us, we feel compelled to love people without limiting our love to relationships we think will last.

As young newlyweds, we sought a way to serve the community together, and foster parenting fit well. Honestly, the "perfect" time to have dependent little human beings suddenly appear in your life never comes, yet foster care serves a critical role in nearly every community.

Looking back, we realize that we didn't overthink the decision to foster. Worrying about future details or complications could have persuaded us not to try. Instead, we experienced the joy and sorrow of parenting twenty-two foster children and all the life each one brought to our home. We would not "redo" life without any of the children who entered our sphere, even with the chaos of the foster care system itself or the exhaustion of keeping up with children who need so much.

Foster parenting felt like a sacred endeavor. When we opened our home to provide for the needs of children, our understanding of the Kingdom of God and the Holy Spirit grew. The Holy Spirit serves in the world to rescue, restore, and cultivate healing. We sensed our actions were similar to the role of the Holy Spirit, and we also felt like partners with Him. He loves and protects those who do not always love in return and who may very well leave Him. When we foster-parented, our physical actions reflected a practical extension of God's love.

Of course, Christianity is not a prerequisite for foster parenting, and we recognize that others have different reasons they choose to foster parent. A strong sense of justice, commitment to community, wanting to "pay forward" how neighbors helped them in the past, and empathy also create desires to help raise children. Others choose to foster before adopting children.

Each foster parent's experience is unique. Not only are all children distinct, but policies differ between states. We wrote our story through several foster cases in order to give the reader an inside view and inspire participation in this cause. We are not authorities on all things related to foster care. We altered identifying details (like names or ages) and maintain confidentiality, but we stayed as true to our days as possible.

We hope to give a raw look into the world of foster care, which is an often invisible, complex reality for approximately four hundred thousand American children at any given time.

Throughout the book, TJ's and Jenn's voices will alternate, since our perspectives are different, and we think it's good to know from whom the thought is originating.

This journey is close to our heart, and we feel exposed sharing it. We hope you'll read it in good faith knowing our intent is to support, encourage, and motivate individuals to care for some of our most vulnerable neighbors.

— *TJ and Jenn*

*This book is a work of non-fiction, with names and identifying details changed to maintain confidentiality.

Chapter 1

In the Beginning

"There are risks and costs to a program of action. But they are far less than the long-range risks and costs of comfortable inaction."
— **John F. Kennedy**[1]

Jenn

I propped up in bed at 4 a.m. as a swaddled ten-pound baby suckled down her bottle, taking split-second breaks to breathe, and I smiled down at her. Upstairs, two preschoolers who kept me going at full-speed throughout the day now slept soundly. Down the hall, two middle-schoolers snored, whom I'd wake up in less than two hours to start their rush to the bus. When my husband TJ had called me at ten the night before, I had asked him what he thought about our Little

Mermaid theme for the kids' Halloween costumes. He had just finished another night's work in combat in Afghanistan, and he chuckled, "As long as no one is Ursula, it'll be cute. And don't spend a fortune on costumes." I yawned as the bottle emptied, thinking through how I would make a little Flounder costume, and thought in wonder, "How did I get here?"

When TJ and I married, we dreamt about what we would do with our lives together. My husband and I met as West Point cadets in 2004. After nearly a school year of teaching Sunday school together, we started running in the mornings. By the following Christmas, we married—a fresh second lieutenant and his teenage bride. I had resigned from West Point, knowing a marriage between two army officers at the height of war was not what we wanted. I made the switch from future officer to army wife.

While we dated, TJ brought up the concept that if we would marry, then God could use us to do greater ministry together than He could with either of us independently. This theory became a pillar of our relationship. Together, we would use our marriage to further the kingdom of God. Sounds romantic, right? Now as I write with ten years of hindsight, serving alongside TJ made me fall in love with him again and again.

After we married, we brainstormed how I should spend my time, since I essentially ripped up my ten-year plan when I left the military academy. I highly valued public service, and, once the activity surrounding the wedding and honeymoon tapered off, I felt eager to embrace a new adventure. I took classes to finish my college degree in counseling, but I felt out of place and wondered what my role was. More importantly, I wondered if this idea of leveraging our marriage for a greater good could really work.

TJ

Jenn and I married in the midst of my time in flight school. Learning to fly helicopters while also figuring out how to love my wife was about all I could handle. I spent my days scaring instructor pilots with self-created flight maneuvers and my evenings with Jenn, romantically memorizing emergency flight procedures together. I expected to deploy for at least a year to Iraq or Afghanistan shortly after graduating flight school, so we embraced this season of relative calm.

Just over seven months after our wedding day, we moved to a new post and linked up with a group of fellow Christians who really challenged me on the concept of discipleship. Discipleship is nothing more than trying to help Christians grow in their faith, to become disciples of Jesus Christ. Prior to this season of life, I made little effort to help others become more like Jesus. I read the Bible and believed it, but I had not intentionally practiced Jesus' command to "Go and make disciples" (Matthew 28:19,20). Honestly, I was initially skeptical of some of the things I heard from these new friends, but their assertions were grounded in Scripture and backed by Jesus' actions during His ministry here on earth. After several white board diagrams and long discussions, I realized not every Christian needed to do the exact same thing, but we all should seek to show the love Christ in some manner.

Through this revelation, I felt our marriage needed a stronger focus on advancing the kingdom of God. Sure, we attended church and a Bible study. I tried to love others in the workplace and Jenn volunteered at pregnancy centers and rescue missions, but were we impacting the world around us as much as we could?

We particularly valued putting our faith into action to care for those most vulnerable in our society. Many areas of Scripture speak to this, but one really stood out to me. James wrote, "Religion that God our Father accepts as pure and faultless is this: to look after orphans and widows in their distress and to keep oneself from being polluted by the world" (James 1:27). Hundreds of children in my city lived in distress. What could I do to help them?

Jenn

I think the idea of fostering came to us because we both had some exposure to the foster care system. TJ's parents fostered children for a large portion of his childhood. As a foster sibling, he saw firsthand the ins and outs of foster care. He witnessed little children coming into his home with significant speech delays or traumas from abuse but, shortly thereafter, grow into healthy playmates. His parents stopped officially fostering when their niece died in a car accident, leaving her three little boys without parents. The three boys moved into TJ's home.

I had less experience with foster care. In high school, I volunteered several hours a week at a temporary teen shelter. I learned the dynamics of group homes and of their necessity due to a chronic shortage of foster families. Mostly, I just interacted with peers since the shelter housed both runaway teens and foster youth. Additionally, my parents invited a teenage girl who needed a stable home life to move into my old room shortly after I married.

Our parents raised us with an understanding that you care for people when you can, and let others care for you, too, when needed. This caring creates community. We saw through our parents' lives what a life of living for others looked like. This familiarity helped us overcome apprehensions and feel confident we could make a positive difference in the community.

Neither of us sensed a voice from God calling us into foster parenting. Just like readers can see God's hand in the story of Esther without mention of His name, we knew He guided us. As we moved ahead, we had no idea what a profound impact foster parenting would have on us emotionally, spiritually, and physically. Being young and naïve has advantages: we knew parenting required sacrifice, in theory, but we could not comprehend the demands of becoming round-the-clock caretakers of neglected children at a moment's notice. We couldn't fathom the cost.

The process in becoming foster parents started by calling the county office and leaving a voicemail stating we wanted to volunteer. A woman returned the call a week later and invited us to an evening meeting to answer questions. At the meeting, a woman in a suit made clear to a group of about forty people that if we missed a training class we would have to start over, and after training, we would complete a long application, go through screens of referrals, interviews, drug tests, and background checks. Then, we must prove our home was ready to host children, complete with fire extinguishers, beds, food, lower water temperatures, and poisons out of reach. She stated firmly, "This is not a job. You will not make money, and this is not adoption. These children are coming with issues."

Great. Sign us up. And don't try a job in sales.

TJ

The first big step in foster parenting is training, but training takes time, and I rarely desire to give up my free time. Additionally, training doesn't feel like it's actually helping anyone, so the first step to becoming a foster parent feels costly with no reward.

I went straight from work to foster parent training with Jenn and some other couples for three hours a night each week for months and then completed a tedious application process—just for the opportunity to help an unknown face. Perhaps this high barrier to entry is important, but it also discourages a lot of people. Thankfully, God kept this service opportunity in the forefront of our minds. The process of qualifying to become a foster parent, with all its requirements, felt like trying to negotiate the Indoor Obstacle Course Test at West Point. (Look this experience up on the Internet if you're not familiar).

Jenn

The lead trainer began each session with potluck-style dinner and games for everyone in the room to get to know one another. We met and trained with about six couples and four single women, all of them decades older than we were. Tracy and Bruce had adopted several years ago from foster care and needed to attend the training to adopt again. A grandfather-aged man named Smoky cackled at the games and silently reclined back through the teaching times. Miss Milly brought the best mashed potatoes, constantly glowed with a loving grin, and voiced her commitment to her neighborhood with passion.

During ten, three-hour long trainings, we learned about the process of foster care and that children only come into foster care as a last resort. An investigator must convince a judge that a child is in danger of severe harm in order to remove a child from his parents.[2] Ongoing reports of neglect or mistreatment must be present, and other methods of assistance like a social worker providing free housing, food, or daycare often go on for months prior to removing a child from his or her legal guardian. Most birth parents lack resources, do not understand acceptable parenting, and have no one else in their lives (like a grandmother) to help with the children. Hunger, homelessness, and poverty are often involved, but these alone are not sufficient grounds for removing children from their parents.

We learned about the state's expectations of us. Foster parenting entails opening one's home and life to co-parent children. At a minimum, the state expects parents to provide food, shelter, and safety. On the surface and in the parents' hearts, the kids become the foster parents' kids for a while. Foster parents shop for, nurture, make dentist appointments, dress, assign chores, feed, coach, teach prayers, bake cakes, help with homework, kiss goodnight—they parent these children. The government intentionally named foster parents as the role parent rather than caregiver out of the recognition that children thrive when they have specific parents, not just adults monitoring them.

They reiterated foster parenting as volunteerism. Most foster parents have full-time jobs in the community (though a few private organizations hire house-parents so foster parents can parent full time). The state reimburses families for certain expenses, including a daily rate set between $13 and $22 a day. While this amount is less than the expense of boarding a dog for a day, the state is leery of raising reimbursement rates out of concern it will incentivize the wrong motives.[3]

Besides these system details, we also received suggestions for how to parent children coming from difficult circumstances. We heard about best practices for making children feel welcome, alternative discipline techniques, and resources for educational support. We were briefed on restrictions like not cutting hair without approval and background checks for babysitters.

TJ

After completing our initial training, we faced the application process. The application to foster is pretty detailed and reaches into nearly every aspect of the foster parents' lives: financial statements, marriage license, personal references, childhood background, dating and fertility history, motives, social security numbers, birth certificates, and driver's licenses. We provided all of these to the home-study professional who interviewed us about some of them, but, overall, the process wasn't terrible. The thoroughness of the application also ensures the state performs its due diligence in vetting us, in case of future problems. We had the doctor verify our health, peed in a cup to prove we're drug free, inked our fingers for the FBI, and hosted the health department to inspect our sewer.

And then we waited. The home-study professional had to input all of this into her system and send it out for a few signatures. About eight weeks later, we received a phone call enthusiastically proclaiming, "You're certified!"

Takeaways

Perhaps the most important decision we made early in our marriage was the choice to leverage our collective gifts to further the kingdom of God. Many people marry thinking it will make them happy or their spouse will fulfill their every need. Any newlywed can testify to the fallacy of this thinking. One of the paradoxes of Christianity is that life on earth is most fulfilling when we serve God and serve others. After all, divorce rates are proof enough that seeking happiness through marriage rarely succeeds.

Foster parenting represents one way to serve God by helping distressed children. We did not have to move across the globe or make a lifelong commitment; it was simply an opportunity to obey God and love our neighbor. Fostering presented us with the chance to help society and strengthen our community right where we lived. It was a practical and life-changing decision, which we never regretted.

Chapter 2
"Yes."

"Strange is our situation here on earth. Each of us comes for a short visit, not knowing why, yet sometimes seeming to divine a purpose. From the standpoint of daily life, however, there is one thing we do know: that man is here for the sake of other men."
—Albert Einstein[4]

Jenn

Police found them alone in their home after responding to a call from a concerned neighbor. They found the eldest child first, at four years old, tied to the kitchen table with a leash-like rope and shortly thereafter discovered a toddler and an infant. The three children rode in the back of a patrol car to a shelter, but the staff realized the shelter could not meet all their needs. The baby went to the hospital where they treated him for pneumonia, and the shelter staff offered to keep the others through the weekend until the Department of Children Services could find a home.

I was twenty-two at the time. I had never cared for kids beyond an occasional babysitting gig, and those kids came with instructions, good health, and returning parents. But TJ and I didn't hesitate or have doubts of inadequacy. They called and needed us. Of course, we said yes. We had just worked our tails off to certify. I'd recently changed my final college credits to online courses, which helped facilitate our ability to take this sort of placement with no notice.

A social worker brought them to our home only a few hours after the call to scribble our signatures giving us custody, drop a duffle bag of belongings, and tell us "Kayla, Nick, and Eddie will be with you indefinitely." Then she smiled and drove off. TJ and I squatted on the ground with a few toys, smiling at six little wide eyes. In those quiet first few minutes, they joined us on the living room floor, making cars "vroom" and trains "choo choo." Nick sat on Eddie's finger, and, as Eddie started to cry, I picked him up to comfort him on my lap. When Kayla saw this, her face became timid, and she withdrew and hid behind the TV in the corner. TJ tried to coax her back into playing, but she was done.

We recognized the many changes the children were adjusting to and understood they may need some space. I think Kayla saw me as stealing her role when I comforted Eddie. I left to fix dinner and get the table set up for the kids to eat. Our first meal turned into a great activity with the first giggles we heard. They happily devoured everything on their plates and received second helpings. I hoped to have the children cleaned up and in pajamas for a bedtime of eight o'clock, but their nervous energy kept them so spry that playing seemed like a better idea than enforcing a new bedtime.

Without children of our own, we had little in the way of kid's stuff waiting for them. We could have received a call for infants through teenagers—boys or girls—so we couldn't stock up for every possibility. We assumed when the social worker said the kids would be with us "indefinitely" she meant a year or so (although the national average ranges around twenty-three months).[5] We had arrived in the area less than a year ago, so we didn't know people in the church very well nor had we told them we anticipated having foster children. Yet, when we shared with them about the kids, they were quick to offer help.

TJ

Our church's response floored us. Perhaps the most obvious and immediate support was meeting the children's physical needs. Within days, our church family brought diapers, clothes, meals, a double stroller, toys, and sippy cups. They emphasized, "Anything you need. Let us know." Their incredible generosity toward us, a couple they hardly knew, surprised us. It was not uncommon for our door bell to ring and then meet people we had never spoken to before who were bringing a box full of provisions or a meal.

Not only did our church help with the children's physical needs, they also offered incredible spiritual support. Our Sunday school class asked how they could pray for us and then kept us in their prayers during the week. The children basked in the love and affection displayed by many members of our church, even though they had never met. We experienced a combination of physical and spiritual support from the church we had never expected, but it made a huge impact on not only Jenn and me, but also the children.

Jenn

Doctor appointments and case meetings, mixed with playing, crying, time-outs, and laughter consumed my days for the next couple weeks. I spent evenings comforting fears, administering breathing treatments for little Eddie's pneumonia, and praying.

Eddie kept crying at night, so I rocked him, sang lullabies, and performed those breathing treatments. I even drove out in the wee hours of the morning to the drug store for some teething medicine—fussy baby in tow. Surely this would help. After a couple more nights of being up through the night, TJ suggested, "Just try feeding him a bottle."

I replied tapping on the book in front of me, "No, TJ, the Caring for Children Birth to Five textbook says babies stop taking bottles at night at like three months old."

TJ reiterated, "Just try it."

Worked like a charm.

Who knew that some babies still took bottles in the middle of the night? Not this mama! This little guy was feeling sick, waking up in a strange place, and now not getting his evening fix? Poor baby. Offer a bottle—now in my bag of tricks.

Late into the first week, we realized from Kayla, and confirmed in hospital documents, that the state told us the wrong name for her brother. Nick was actually Nike—like the shoe. We hoped having the wrong name on custody papers wouldn't cause issues.

Kayla and Nike's lack of basic communication skills and age-appropriate behavior shocked me. The children displayed deficient knowledge related to basic words, numbers, and colors while also lacking skills like potty training, sharing, and playing with toys. I sat stunned watching two-year-old Nike inhale food as if he had never eaten before or might not eat again. Then I remembered how they had spent their days alone, and patiently, but immediately, started teaching these things.

Just about the time we started to find our rhythm of names, needs, and routines—it all changed. The children and I ran errands together an hour before a scheduled visit with their birth mom. I remember sitting in an orientation with the gym daycare ladies so that I could finally start using the gym daycare and exercising after two weeks of pent-up energy. I fumbled around under the stroller to find my ringing phone in the abyss of my purse, and the voice on the phone said, "Hi, Mrs. Menn. Please have their bags packed when the children are picked up for the visit, as they'll be moving to an aunt out of state. Have them ready at the scheduled pick-up time." Like in an hour?!

I excused us from the orientation and rushed home, fighting back tears of astonishment more than sadness. An hour later, a county transportation worker I had never met stuffed the children's belongings in her messy trunk, buckled the little ones in, closed the doors, and drove off. And then they were gone. As suddenly as it started, it all came to a screeching halt.

TJ

Due to a training flight, I missed the opportunity to say goodbye to Kayla, Nike, and Eddie. If I had known the children were leaving, I would have taken the day off from work or changed my flight to enable me to see them off. When I came home after work, the house was clean and eerily quiet—no giggling little ones to hug or wrestle with and no toys scattered around on the living room floor.

Our lives changed dramatically when the kids arrived—going from zero to three children was not easy. However, going from three to zero children felt just as abrupt. The children had only been in our home for a couple weeks, but our lifestyles adapted quickly. It felt like a fast rollercoaster ride.

I wish I could have been there to hug these three children goodbye and comfort them as they moved to another unknown home. I wanted to demonstrate a fatherly presence. I am thankful, however, to have spent the time we did with them, and I take comfort in knowing their Heavenly Father loves each of them more than we ever could.

Jenn

The contrast between playful shouts and the deafening silence of the house brought out anger in me. "Who were they with?" I wondered. "Are they really better off?" I debated in my mind, "What about us? Can't someone acknowledge our part in the kids' lives by involving us in meeting their aunt or schedule the pick-up with more notice?" Even worse, I had this kids' Bible song stuck in my head. So, I grumbled in annoyance as I cleaned up the kitchen, laundry, and toys.

The next day, while stuck in my pitiful attitude, I realized my mind was on replay. I thought, "Jenny, listen to the words of the children's song you keep singing: 'In my Father's house are many mansions, many mansions in my Father's house. I go and prepare a place for you, for you.'" I smiled, knowing the Holy Spirit heard my questions. I looked up the Scripture the lyrics came from and read Jesus' words in John chapter 14, "Do not let your hearts be troubled. Trust in God, trust also in me...I go and prepare a place for you, if it were not so, I would've told you" (John 14:1-2).

Simple, I know, but I needed the reminder of His control in all things. I'm sure a judge considered the legitimacy and background of the aunt. Looking at the situation objectively, having a family member surface after such a short time in care was such a favorable outcome for the kids. The children may have even known her all their lives. I just didn't like being out of control. I served my part to the utmost, which included assuming responsibility for the kids and falling in love quickly. Now, my role became moving forward without a troubled heart, trusting God as an attentive Father.

Takeaways

This whirlwind of changes introduced us to a pattern we continued to experience as foster parents. We start adapting to little ones quickly while running all over town for appointments, responding to surprising behaviors, and juggling the coexisting feelings of joy and exhaustion inherent to parenting. We would find routines, use spare time to catch up their delayed development, feed growing bodies, readjust to short-notice changes, and report to ever-rotating case manager staff. All of this goes on while having no control over case outcomes, absorbing the shock of loss, and trying to prepare for the next call with soon-to-be cherished lives. Some children, like Kayla, Nike, and Eddie, came and went so fast—just two weeks—that the pattern felt like a tornado. We didn't create a deep, emotional bond with the children beyond a fond remembrance, but we believe the stability and love during this time of crisis helped.

While the state and society rightfully focus on the physical needs of children (like clothes, food, and shelter), we believe their spiritual needs are of equal or even greater importance. The love, faith, and hope these children experienced in our home and through the local church is what will make a difference in their lives for eternity. Even though they were only in our care for a few weeks, we believe seeds were sown in their life, which may result in a harvest no one can see until heaven. Physical needs are still important; indeed, they are often the mechanisms through which spiritual values are expressed.

Kayla, Nike, and Eddie suffered the repercussions of their parents' poor decisions, and the experience certainly shaped their lives for years to come. We know the children felt loved and cherished while they were in our home and with our church family. Kayla's skittish fear when she arrived morphed into hugs and giving sassy older-sister directions to the boys. If Nike knew love through food, his tank left full. Eddie snuggled for much of the day, and the mimicking faces and sounds during dinnertime surely added up to a sense of belonging. Sometimes, foster parents are only there to provide a loving environment to facilitate the transition to other arrangements, and this was our experience with this case. We have never heard from any of the children or anything further about their situation.

Chapter 3

Harmony

"Spiritual warfare is very real. There is a furious, fierce, and ferocious battle raging in the realm of the spirit between the forces of God and the forces of evil. Warfare happens every day, all the time. Whether you believe it or not, you are in a battlefield."
—**Pedro Okoro**[6]

"Let's wake up from our deceptive slumber and open our eyes to the fact that Satan is the one behind every childhood victimization."
—**Beth Moore**[7]

Jenn

Before we could reflect too much on Kayla, Eddie, and Nike, our house filled up with different children. A case manager greeted me cheerfully on the phone and relayed the only information she had, "Harmony is a white newborn and needs to be picked up at Longwind hospital at 11:00 a.m. Do you want to take her?"

"Does she have any siblings?" I asked.

"I don't know," she replied.

"How long do you expect she'll be with us?"

"I don't know."

"Has she been exposed to drugs?"

"Yes, cocaine, but I do not know of any medical complications."

Being a Saturday morning, TJ was home and heard the conversation. We asked the case manager for a few minutes to pray together, since sometimes the Holy Spirit will bring a Word to mind or a strong sense in one direction. When we didn't feel any hesitation, we returned the call and gladly said "Yes."

So, there we were, eleven in the morning, at Longwind with Harmony, as the discharge nurse explained how to care for a newborn for forty minutes. At the end, she asked, "Any questions?"

TJ, in his typical weekend attire of a John Deere sweatshirt, cowboy boots, and baseball hat, began with, "So this may sound like a stupid question…"

The nurse assured us, "No, no, no. No such thing as a stupid question."

TJ, obviously hesitant, asked, "Is she white?"

Even my eyes went wide. "Of all the questions!" I thought. Because here we were standing over a little black baby, who clearly had dark skin. The nurse gave us a blank look and tilted her head. Her face betrayed her thoughts, "Uh, oh—a stupid question."

"Um, no. Is that a problem, sir?" The nurse questioned.

TJ quickly replied, "No, not at all. We were told to come pick up a white baby. I just want to make sure we have the right baby. No problem at all."

A few minutes passed while we waited for the social worker to arrive with the papers to sign, and Harmony rocked the "car seat challenge" required to take her home. (This is a test where the infant sits in the car seat for a period of time and nurses check to make sure the baby can breathe before allowing the child to depart the hospital.)

We heard a little *pst pst pst pst pst* in the background that caught our attention. A social worker (who happened to be African-American) said to TJ and I gently, "So I hear you have a problem with the child being black. Are you still willing to take her?"

As if leaving the hospital with someone else's child wasn't awkward enough, we spent a few uncomfortable moments defending our racial openness before we were on our way home with our very first newborn. TJ had never driven home as carefully as he did that day.

Beyond the occasional baby holding, I had never cared for an infant before Harmony. Like all little ones, her precious first days had a constant rhythm of eating and sleeping. I cherished the slow and quiet hours I spent adoring her, especially after our last wild placement. She had cocaine in her system, but I couldn't tell the difference between typical baby cries and those from drug withdrawal. She seemed to develop just fine in my oh-so-expert perspective.

TJ

Although Harmony was the first newborn we had ever cared for, she was this particular mother's eighth child. In fact, the mother lost her right to parent the previous seven children, but the state gave her another chance to raise Harmony.

I found this situation particularly upsetting because the parents desired to control many aspects of the case without changing their own behavior. Most of the time we found birth parents pretty understanding when we desired to travel with the children out of state for major holidays like Christmas or Thanksgiving, as long as we did not interfere with their visits. Since the children are in the custody of the state, the birth parents technically do not have a say in the care of the children, but the state tries to accommodate parents' wishes in matters pertaining to travel or other seemingly minor issues.

In this particular instance, we wanted to travel to my parents' for Christmas, but Harmony's parents did not want us to take her outside the state's borders. Jenn didn't want to leave Harmony, but she also didn't want to miss out on the opportunity to see friends and family over the Christmas holiday. I really wanted to head back to the farm and assured Jenn that Harmony would be just fine in respite care. The parents had waited until just a couple weeks before Christmas to voice their objection, which was another reason why their decision annoyed me. After about a week of debating back and forth, Jenn agreed to place Harmony in respite care with another foster parent, and we left with the assurances of the case manager about Harmony's well-being ringing in our ears.

Not even ten days later, we returned to find Harmony very sick, along with a case of diaper rash so severe that it looked like open sores. We were upset not only with the foster parent who had allowed this to happen (an elderly single woman, whose home was investigated after this incident), but also with the state and her parents for refusing to allow us to take Harmony on our trip.

Our nation has many loving foster parents, and the state intends for foster care to provide children with an opportunity to thrive. Ideally, foster parents model healthy relationships, right living, and offer continual support. Birth parents can also benefit from a wide variety of services while their children are in foster care. However, some individuals choose to become foster parents for a stream of income rather than to parent. The government mostly considers only safety and well-being as the two major criteria in foster care programs. A person is eligible to foster parent if they complete the training and can offer a bed, shelter, and protection from crime. The relatively low standard for foster home certification leaves many foster children living in poverty with adults who offer little sense of belonging to the family, devote no time advocating for them, provide no availability for extra-curricular activities, and no vehicle to access community resources.[8]

Refusing to allow us to take Harmony with us represented one of the first times we disagreed with the state over the child's best interest; unfortunately, it would not be the last.

Jenn

As we learned about Harmony's parents, the situation looked bleak. Several of her seven older siblings were already in jail. Her mom lost rights to all of them. If Harmony had the same dad, the court may have terminated the parents' rights shortly after her birth. However, a new guy means a new try.

Her mom stayed engaged with the case plan, even though the birth dad didn't. I sent an encouraging note to every weekly visitation, and her mom often wrote back. Oftentimes, I drove Harmony to the visits and took joy in seeing her mom smile over Harmony in her arms. Still, I knew from the case manager that her life outside of visitation hadn't changed. Still doing drugs. Still jobless. Still suffering from and engaging in domestic violence.

TJ

One of the most powerful things we do for the children entering our home is to pray for them and their parents. Obviously, meeting their physical and emotional needs is crucial, but we have a distinct privilege to pray for their spiritual health and protection.

We spent a lot of time praying for Harmony. Spiritual warfare is real and is raging all around us. When you read the quotes at the beginning of the chapter, you probably didn't think twice about the implications of them upon your life. Even as I write this, I wonder if people will think I'm a lunatic for actually believing things take place in our world we cannot see, taste, smell, touch, or hear with our physical senses. The repercussions of angelic and demonic activity surface in our physical world every minute of every day.

Harmony's presence in our life was a wonderful blessing, and she will always have a special place in my heart. Among other reasons, I think God placed her in our lives to teach us about the spiritual struggle and the importance of prayer.

Very late one evening after I fed Harmony, I sat in our rocking chair, trying to coax her to fall asleep. Her dark brown eyes searched my face as I told her some of the things my mom had always told me. The Old Testament patriarchs used to bless their children, and I think the spoken word has power. I remember my mom consistently telling me, "God's going to really use you someday." I believed it then, and I still believe it to this day.

As I was talking to Harmony and marveling at the beautiful little girl God created, I felt the presence of evil enter the room. It was eerie. Chills ran through my body. In fact, even as I write this several years later, I have chills running down my spine. Harmony also sensed it, I believe, as her face contorted in a manner I had never seen before. I panicked, and did the only thing I could think to do—pray.

I began praying fervently and audibly, asking God to protect this child. I asked Him to take care of her, to love her, to shelter her, and I asked all of it in the name of Jesus. At the conclusion of these prayers, I still did not feel a peace. I continued to pray for God's protection over our home, for our marriage, and for Him to keep us free from evil and to heal Harmony from any lasting drug effects or pain she may have experienced. I asked for God to break any generational strongholds that would draw her into harmful behavior during her life. I repeated Jesus' name again and again while I asked Him to bless her, to protect her spiritually, and to watch over her all her life. Eventually, the tension passed, Harmony's face relaxed, and she fell into a deep and peaceful sleep.

Whether or not anything spiritually significant occurred in Harmony's life that night, I don't know, but I know the experience changed mine. While some people may believe in the theoretical idea of spiritual warfare, I am convinced it exists and shapes more of our physical world than we are comfortable to admit. It is certainly more than an abstract idea or philosophical theory. God used this occasion to strengthen my faith and demonstrate to me the reality of spiritual warfare in the little lives we served.

Jenn

Around this time, the army ordered TJ to move out of state for a long training. At that point, Harmony's case still had months—if not years—left before courts would determine whether to place her back with family or for adoption. If a parent shows some progress, like attending visits, the state has to keep making efforts to bring the family together. So my staying back for Harmony while TJ moved would cause an indefinite separation. Instead, we gave her case manager a couple months' notice so she could find a great placement for her.

When a kind, smiling, chatty retired couple who had fostered only babies for decades came to pick her up, a sense of peace blanketed over me that Harmony would be in good hands. They patiently listened as I explained her unique needs and took all her belongings so she'd have familiar clothes and toys—even though they'd cared for dozens of babies and surely had all the knowledge and supplies they wanted. I had typed up a booklet of her usual schedule, doctors, and history. They had my contact information in case they had any questions.

This type of move was easier for everyone to cope with—full of information to ensure the best care of the child and, most importantly of all, not hasty. I appreciated that the case manager let us meet one another and trusted us to handle the transition.

When people in the community found out Harmony was a foster baby and not an adoptive baby, almost everyone's face immediately dropped, and many said, "I could never do that. Doesn't it hurt so bad when they have to go back?"

Yes. That's the answer. Losing a loved one totally hurts. (And, I often want to reply, "Thanks for making me think about it!" while she's in my arms.) But caring for Harmony, whether a day, or a year, or a lifetime, was a blessing. I also consider TJ's discussion of prayer. Maybe God simply wanted her to be in our arms for a season to pray over her, to loosen chains of injustice. We continue to pray for her.

Harmony eventually came up for adoption two years later, like the seven siblings preceding her. Her foster parents, the older couple whom I met, had to fight for her in court because the case manager thought they were too old to keep her. Thankfully, they adopted her. We have not maintained contact with Harmony. I think if we remained in the same city we would, but our relocation made it especially difficult.

Takeaways

Harmony's mother's behavior made this case extremely difficult to balance. On the one hand, we desire to see people overcome their past difficulties, defeat their addictions, and become responsible, loving parents. On the other hand, when individuals make the same mistake over and over again, it places a huge burden on their children and society.

This case also taught us a lot about foster children who entered state custody and were not reunited with either a family member or their parents. When children enter foster care, the state assumes legal guardianship, hopefully just temporarily. The fewer orphans the better, as long as those children can reunite with their family safely and assure their well-being. Of the four hundred thousand foster children, two thirds wait in limbo to possibly return to their birth family. And the vast majority of them will.

Foster children may have adoptive plans made for them, the foster home may even be considered a pre-adoptive home, but this does not mean foster parents will have the chance to adopt the kids living in their home. Alternatively, foster parents are never required to adopt their foster children.

The children who do come up for adoption have had their parents' guardian rights permanently removed because of unchanged risk of abuse, abandonment, or neglect. These kids wait for adoption by families.[9] For those waiting for adoption, some stay with their foster family who end up becoming their adoptive family, and others are matched with a waiting adoptive family.

A lot of children in foster care all over the country need adoptive homes. Only about a third of the children in need of adoptive homes end up in families each year. Think about that: out of ten children wanting and waiting for a mom and dad, only three find a family. (The resource page in the appendix has more information on how to adopt or foster.)

A lack of families is not the only reason children linger in foster care. Some children have adoptive families that want them, but a case manager decides it's not the "best fit" for the child. Certain bureaucratic regulations make it difficult to apply individual considerations to a case. Furthermore, moving children between state borders can take years. Still other children fare well in foster care and do not require a lot of attention, so the case continues for month after month without any forward movement toward a permanent solution, while their case manager faces other "more urgent" needs. We heard supervisors often excuse delays on routine progression as, "The squeaky wheel gets the grease around here."

Chapter 4

Moving In and On

"The important work of moving the world forward does not wait to be done by perfect men."
— **George Eliot** [10]

Jenn

I already mentioned the general shortage of foster families nationwide. When families in the community won't take in children, they live in children's shelters, or sometimes older youth live in apartment situations, preparing them for independent living without a family. Of course, case managers are constantly looking for family homes, so when Harmony was about four weeks old, we received a plea to care for more.

Like two peas in a pod, Shelly and Holly arrived, undersized for their age and attached at the hip. At five and seven years old, they held hands and smiled nervously with a backpack full of their toys and schoolwork as big as they were. We greeted them at the social worker's car in our driveway. After introductions, I asked, "Would you like to come in for a snack and see your bedroom?" They silently nodded in unison and quickly walked to their bedroom. They lit up with smiles and hugged each other before even dropping their bags. The room had no fancy decorations. They just realized they would be together. TJ stayed with the social worker to complete the paperwork without the girls having to watch and wait.

The girls came to us from a children's shelter called Heart Home. There, they stayed in different rooms, but sometimes the staff let Shelly go say goodnight to Holly, and they usually sat together at dinner. In our home, they set up tea parties, raked leaves into piles and jumped around, read books cuddled under blankets, and slept in a queen-sized bed together.[11] The only time they spent apart was in the classroom, like most siblings. In the history of the world, you won't find sweeter sisters than Shelly and Holly, I promise.

We welcomed Shelly and Holly into our home, recognizing they would only live with us for a few months. We already knew the army was moving us six months later across the country. But the girls had no better option.

They stayed in a local shelter because their baby brother tested positive for cocaine at birth. This prompted an investigation into the other children's welfare, which resulted in all three children coming into state custody. Their baby brother went to a foster family unable to care for all three siblings. Shelly and Holly still hadn't met him one month later. The Department of Child Services couldn't find another foster home for them, so after they sat in an office all day nervously playing with a doll, a social worker drove them to the shelter.

When a case manager asked us about the girls, we all agreed the best idea was to keep the girls together, even if just for the six months we had left in the area. Going back home to their mom didn't look promising since she had already dropped out of rehab. Their dad, who had not lived with them, seemed to care for the girls, but had major obstacles to overcome. While the girls lived with us, case managers sought a long-term placement for all three siblings.

Right away, we invited the foster family with their baby brother over to our home to meet the girls. Shelly and Holly adored holding their little brother and tried to make him smile. They spoke baby talk to him, we took pictures, and then they went off to play with their Barbies without signs of sadness when he had to go. I kept in touch with their baby brother's foster parents. We spoke regularly on the phone, and I would often share stories about how the girls were doing. TJ and I prayed diligently for this family to offer to take the girls when we moved in May.

In the meantime, we played. Our role was to make the girls' life seem as typical as possible. God timed their placement perfectly, as they came just ten days before a scheduled vacation. Since TJ wasn't at work all day, the time they spent with him in the beginning of the placement formed a stronger bond than if he had been home only in the mornings and evenings.

TJ

The girls took a little while to warm up to me. Coming from a fatherless home, they really hadn't had much contact with adult men in their lives to this point. While a loving mother can parent a child well without a father, God naturally designed children to have a father and mother in their family.

Like the majority of foster children, Shelly and Holly did not have a father active in their life, and they craved a male role model.[12] Girls and boys both need strong, compassionate, loving men engaged in their life to help fashion their identity as children of God. They need a male role model of what commitment, discipline, and self-sacrifice looks like.

Perhaps the best impetus for building our relationship was a long-weekend vacation to a local beach house, which a generous citizen donated to soldiers who had returned from Iraq or Afghanistan in the last year. The girls and I bonded on this trip because we spent a lot of uninterrupted time together.

Dressing up at the children's museum, chasing birds at the beach, and eating Mickey Mouse pancakes helped form our identity as a family. These moments also represented opportunities to establish behavioral norms and clarify expectations. As the girls role-played in the children's museum, we saw some of their hopes and dreams for the future. The five of us played on the beach without the interruptions of phone calls, emails, or television. In restaurants, we talked about appropriate table manners and discussed some of the girls' favorite things. The trip was great because we spent time getting to know each other without the distractions of daily life. It amounted to spending a lot of quality time with the girls and helped ease their transition into our home and our lives.

Jenn

Once we returned home, the girls enrolled in their new school, picked chores and rewards they would like, and we settled into a routine. They interacted with Harmony well. After a couple weeks, I think they realized they would stay awhile. Holly tugged on my arm while I cooked supper one night.

"Can I call you 'mommy'?" she asked. "No one at Heart Home would let me call them 'mom.'"

I answered, "Yes, baby girl. You can call me 'mom' or 'Jenny,' whichever you like." She hugged my side and ran off to play. I smiled and went back to stirring.

Both girls constantly made observations about the world around them. Shelly asked questions by the minute and stayed up late to read books (her favorite being knock-knock jokes and a princess Bible). Shelly also helped Holly practice her reading after she finished her own homework. I felt such joy experiencing all the firsts with little Holly like tying her shoes, learning to swim, riding a bike, and teaching her to read.

Months passed with lighthearted life. We sang karaoke, danced like ballerinas, and played soldiers. Our day-to-day life looked like a happy American family of five.

Shelly sang all the time. One of my favorite parts of the day was the few minutes before we walked to school. Shelly woke up and got ready quickly. She played on her scooter outside while the rest of us finished up (usually as Holly took the ten minutes to tie her shoes and I loaded Harmony into a sling on me). I could hear Shelly singing through the open windows, "Savior! He can move the mountains; my God is mighty to save. He is mighty to save."

One morning, as I walked Shelly into her second grade class, her teacher pulled me aside, "Mrs. Menn, Shelly has been such a joy to have in class. She is my sunshine on a hard day. Yesterday, the class was rowdy, and I made them have silent time. A few moments later, Shelly came up to my desk. At first, I was upset because of the class, so I turned her away. Shelly looked disappointed, so I said, 'Wait, what is it, Shelly?' She just left a note and hurried back to her desk. The note said, 'Don't worry Mrs. Jamison, I'll always be good for you.'"

I'm telling you—they're angels.

We had a lot of fun on our walks to school in the morning. We enjoyed playing games like "I Spy," racing, learning songs, and just talking about things on their minds. One morning, it smelled like someone was frying food.

Holly said, "Mmmm. Smells like french fries."

Shelly answered, "Someone must be eating french fries for breakfast."

I chimed in, "Yuck, french fries for breakfast? I wouldn't want that!"

"Why? God eats french fries for breakfast," Holly stated.

"Umm, I don't know about that. I don't think God is up in heaven eating french fries for breakfast. He's got better stuff up there," I reasoned.

Holly insisted, "No, really. I know He's eating them."

"How do you know He's eating them?" I asked.

Holly answered very matter-of-factly, "Because I can smell it!"

Besides singing, Shelly wrote songs. One she entitled, "God Is the Perfect One." I encouraged her to write it down, and we recorded it on my computer. It goes like this:

God is the perfect one to love. He is the perfect one above. Why won't you see? He is the one you should love. Yeah, yeah, yeah. I love Him the way He loves me. Why can't you see? Oh, why can't you see? He is the best one you should love forever and ever long above. I love Him, oh, yes, I love Him.

Another chorus she wrote the first week she came into foster care at the children's shelter is below.

Don't listen to the devil; listen to the angels; follow your heart and don't be scared of me. I'm sorry. I'm sorrrrry. Don't be scared of me. I'm sorrrry.

When I asked her why the song said "I'm sorry," she said the song was like God was singing it to her. These sweet lyrics remind me that God is so present with the fatherless. He sings over them. Friends who grew up in foster care share similar memories of how closely God walked with them in the midst of hardship—even those who had not ever been taught about Him.

TJ

When the girls came to us, we really only knew their ages and their mom's struggle with drugs. Well, the information about their ages was off by a year, but it was close. In the next few weeks, we learned more details about the case and met both parents. Usually, a case manager pulls together every adult who is involved with the children and has an initial team meeting to share the plan ahead. These meetings provided insight into the children's past and helped us better relate to the girls.

Team meetings are usually held early in the case, but they are certainly not the only gatherings relevant to the case. Court hearings and case manager meetings are especially important events for foster parents to attend. Court dates tend to bring accountability for the state and the parents, while case manager meetings help keep the team on track. Since we lived with the children, we knew a lot about their current feelings and behaviors, so case managers often asked us to attend these events. Besides advocating for the girls, the gatherings also provided us with a wealth of information about the case's progression.

Reading this section may make it sound as if there are meetings every week, but, in reality, getting all the relevant parties together to discuss a case is pretty difficult. Court hearings are normally six months to a year apart, and case manager meetings are held perhaps once a quarter. Of course, with all the other medical or psychological appointments in the children's life, it can seem more frequent.

It was difficult for both of us to appear at every meeting, but we thought it was important for at least one of us to be present if the other could not make it. Oftentimes, we knew the children better than most—if not all of—the people in the room. Furthermore, these events represented some of the only chances to influence the direction of the case.

Case managers try their best, but they carry the burden of dozens of cases and may only see the children monthly. On more than one occasion, they have confused specific happenings of a case with another case, primarily because of all the other case histories in their minds. They're thinking professionally, whereas we as foster parents tend to think and advocate personally. We believe our presence in court hearings or family team meetings helped decision-makers better understand the complete picture.

Jenn

As we learned Shelly and Holly's story better, we saw the pattern of destruction their family followed. Their mother grew up in and out of foster care and was never placed with an adoptive family, so when she turned a certain age, she was kicked out of the foster care system and told to be independent. She left her younger siblings, still in foster care, found a man to live with, and gave birth shortly thereafter. Eight years later, her younger brother remained in the system. Before they came into foster care, Shelly and Holly's mom had brought them to state-supervised family visits with Uncle Billy, as the girls referred to him. They played together, and he told the girls all kinds of horrible things about being in foster care. Naturally, when the girls ended up in foster care, the stories brought new fear.

One day as we played together in the front yard, Shelly yelled, "Billy!" and ran to embrace a young man. Sure enough, their mother's younger brother Billy, who was now twelve years old, lived in a foster home in our neighborhood. What are the chances?! He soon received an open invitation to come over after school, which he often did. His foster parents told me of his troubles like theft and fights at school, but in our home with his young nieces, Billy played with toys, chased the girls in the yard, ate popsicles, and wrestled around. He felt safe to remove his tough mask around us.

I learned Billy's birthday had recently passed, so I asked his foster parents if we could take him out. On Friday, I swung by to pick him up, and we all went to a "dive-in-movie" at a pool where we watched Ice Age on the big screen while floating in the water and swimming. Afterward, we all sang "Happy Birthday" to Billy, and he proudly blew out his candles.

We lived in a big city with slim chances of crossing paths with Billy. This meeting happened only by the hand of God. Billy received a sense of family as he looked toward a dark future like that of the five siblings who aged out of the system before him. Sometimes, I felt guilty we couldn't take Billy, too—not that anyone asked us. The system did not recognize Billy as family to Shelly, Holly, or their brother, nor did the case manager make arrangements for them to live near one another. But God knew, and He worked providentially to bring them together.

In March, shortly after Billy's party, we received a call out of the blue that the girls would move in two days. The case manager said, "Have their suitcases packed up, and on Sunday I'll move their belongings. On Monday, I'll pick them up after school and bring them to their new family."

The case manager did not, and would not, tell us anything else. She seemed angry that I even asked for further details or the rationale behind the decision. She wouldn't let us drive the girls over or even tell us where they planned to go—so we could tell the girls. Frustrated is an understatement. The girls felt scared, and we had little information to help ease their concerns. We reassured them by reminding them of how fear turned to happiness when they came to us, so surely fun new adventures would come. TJ went in late to work so he could walk with us to school, and we said goodbye to the girls as they crossed the sidewalk into the building. I went home and cried, jaw clenched in anger at the stupid system.

From my experience, when one of our case managers wanted to do something, she cut off any argument by saying her idea was, "What's best for the children." I couldn't understand how such a hasty move was "best for the children." All day, I boiled in frustration while I cleaned up some of the girls' belongings: "Why wouldn't they listen to easing a transition? We still have two months here! I know Shelly. I know she wants to be checked on at night time, to make sure she's okay." I heard the girls' questions and felt responsible for protecting them.

My mom wrote an email that day saying, "I'm praying for you two and for the girls. I prayed for them this morning, and God gave me a picture in my mind's eye. Inside a hallway—could have been a school, I'm not sure—I looked at the back of the girls as they walked down the hallway holding hands. Holly was on the left and Shelly on the right. Then holding each of their hands was what I guess were angels except I really didn't see wings. They wore white robes [and had] beautiful curly hair. One looked down at Holly; the other was looking straight ahead. With it, I thought of the Scripture, 'I have engraved you are in the palm of my hand' (Isaiah 49:16). I know from past experience, when I see someone from behind it usually denotes their future because they stand ahead of me and are moving forward. My thoughts and prayers are with you both today, as well as those sweet girls."

I took heart in this encouragement and trusted God's presence with them. My mom had no idea I had to bring them to school to say goodbye. Part of the way I can love and let go is through this firm belief in the Fatherhood of God, which He continues to reiterate to me in times of distress. When I felt totally out of control for Holly and Shelly's lives and as if they were experiencing injustice, I needed to believe that He actively parents these children, just as His Holy Spirit guides, protects, provides for, and disciplines me. Shelly's songs and my mom's vision both remind me that Jesus Christ sees and knows Holly and Shelly.

That night at nine, I took a phone call from an unknown number. I almost let the call go since I felt emotionally exhausted. The director of a private child placement agency in town with whom we did not foster introduced herself and said, "Mrs. Menn, we have two girls that have been sitting here since after school. Their names are Shelly and Holly, and we have nowhere for them to go tonight. We were wondering—would you take them back?" The case manager had made a mistake. The placement she had planned for the girls already had kids living there with no extra capacity for the girls.

Of course, they came home. Those poor girls had a terribly confusing and frightening day. They arrived hungry because no one fed them supper. Since the case manager had already taken their belongings, each girl changed into one of TJ's t-shirts. We cuddled, read books like always, and thanked God in bedtime prayers.

The comfort I received from God does not make right the mistakes the girls experienced in the child welfare system. What happened unnecessarily hurt us all. Yet, in the midst of injustice, God is intimately present.

The next eight weeks after the girls came back, we sought more involvement in the girls' future plans. No one ever apologized or really acknowledged what happened with the girls leaving and returning. We discussed transition plans at length with the whole case team: the case manager, Court-Appointed Special Advocate (CASA), birth parents, foster parents for the girls' brother, and us. In these meetings, the foster parents of the girls' brother decided they would be willing to take the girls. Praise God!

This time, we planned the move. The new foster mom came and picked up the girls' belongings. She told the girls about how their room would be decorated: Holly's side like her favorite princess and Shelly's like Hannah Montana. Then, she planned to return the next day after she had their belongings settled.

During our last Bible time with the girls in the morning, we read, coincidentally, "The Lord will be with you wherever you go," and the words encouraged and reassured our whole family of God's protection over Shelly and Holly. "Have I not commanded you? Be strong and courageous. Do not be terrified. Do not be discouraged. For the Lord will be with you wherever you go" (Joshua 1:8)

The girls anticipated the move and smiled nervously as they hopped in their new mom's car in our driveway to go home. In the moment, with all honesty, passing these sweet girls over to another mother felt as if my time had been spent in vain. I should've felt relieved at the smoother transition. But the week the girls left, I wrote to a friend: "More than anything except heaven, saying goodbye made me so long for children of our own that we wouldn't have to hand over to someone else after parenting." What was the point?

Soon, I realized I had really asked, "What's in it for me?" Of course the time the girls were with us had met a real need for the girls. My feeling of emptiness felt like vanity when, in reality, the presence of emptiness proved I poured out to them.

God encouraged me through worship. I prayed, "Thank you for using these girls to extend our ministry." Next, I recorded all the ways I saw God work through the girls in our home. God also encouraged me with 1 Corinthians 15:58 which reads, "Therefore, dear brothers, stand firm. Let nothing move you. Always give yourselves fully to the work of the Lord because you know that your labor in the Lord is not in vain."

At this point, I also reflected on the strange way the girls went away and came back. I became thankful rather than pitiful for the opportunity to have a couple more months with the girls.

Shortly after the episode of leaving and returning, Shelly asked questions about baptism out of the blue. Anyone who knew Shelly knew she grasped humanity's sin and God's perfecting love for her in Jesus Christ. So, we let her choose baptism and invited her birth family to join in the ceremony. Her grandmother brought little pearl earrings to the ceremony. If Shelly's baptism is the only reason their time in our home was extended, it would be plenty.

TJ

As I reflect on the time we spent with these girls, I realize I made several mistakes with Shelly and Holly. I sometimes raised my voice, and it scared them. A few times, I lost my patience with them.

However, they loved me not because of my parenting skills, but mostly because I provided a safe, protective presence. They loved to ride on my back, pretending I was a horse or a cow. We played games with army gear or used stuffed animals and dolls in pretend fairy tales. I may have even sat through a pink tea party or two. They just wanted to spend time with me, even if it was riding in the truck on an errand to the home improvement store.

Thankfully, children don't need perfect fathers. Jesus is the only perfect man to ever walk the earth. In fact, oftentimes, children learn a lot from the failures of their parents. But they cannot learn from or even observe an absent father.

These girls represent a success story in my mind. In time, the new foster family adopted the girls along with their little brother, and the kids continue to grow into outstanding young people. Their adoption into a family with a strong marriage and the opportunity to live with their brother epitomize the role Christians should play in our society today. The family continues to serve God by loving needy children. We continue to pray for all the children who have ever entered into our family, as well as those like Billy. I am confident the love and acceptance Shelly and Holly experienced during childhood will break the cycle of their birth parents' destructive choices.

Jenn

We lost contact with the girls the day they left our home. We tried to call and check on them, but those calls started and ended with 'click.' No response. This hurt and frustrated us because we felt that we played a role in helping the placement come together. About four years later, a mutual friend reconnected our families through Facebook. Now, we get to watch the girls grow.

Though I felt irate at being cut out, I now see how our involvement early on in their placement may have been problematic—it could've slowed the girls' bond with their new foster parents and stressed the family. We were just two more people clamoring for visits or attention in addition to birth family, court advocates, and case managers. Being a child in foster care is like being swept up in a storm. It's a time of crisis, and even good things can cause stress or emotional overload. After the storm settles, then the children have the capacity for extra relationships or activities.

Takeaways

God refers to Himself as Father to all those who follow Him, but He singles out the fatherless and assures us He is a "Father to the fatherless," who knows their names, thoughts, and the number of hairs upon their heads (Psalm 68:5). He loves them, and they can rest in Him. He is their anchor.

Our time with these particular girls helped us recognize how important the role of a father is to young children. Foster parenting presents an opportunity for Christian men to love, defend, and protect some of the most marginalized members of our society. These children need an advocate. More often than not, a foster dad may represent the only man in their life who cares for them.

Christian men have an opportunity to help solve this crisis of leadership and, in doing so, impress Christ's love upon an entire generation. Perhaps the love and acceptance children see modeled by their foster fathers today will break the pattern of sinful behavior so firmly established in our society. Indeed, when men of faith sit on society's sidelines, content to watch the world destroy itself, it demonstrates apathy and selfishness. God has entrusted the responsibility of leadership to men, and it is a role God expects men to take seriously.

Chapter 5

The Opposite of Convenience

"Endow us with courage that is born of loyalty to all that is noble and worthy."

— **Cadet Prayer from the United States Military Academy at West Point** [13]

Jenn

After Shelly and Holly moved, we packed up our house into boxes to prepare to move halfway across the country. By the end of the week, we ate off paper plates and dressed out of packed suitcases. Our plans for our last weekend consisted of a farewell party on Friday evening, moving Harmony on Monday, and catching a flight on Tuesday for a quick vacation before coming home to load the moving truck and drive away.

So, of course, we received a call to take an emergency placement Friday afternoon. I stopped putting on my makeup for the night, placed the call on speakerphone, and heard about a young man whose parents both laid in the hospital on their death beds. The children's shelter staff said he needed to leave after acting out aggressively against another child. Phillip had significant autism. He was nonverbal, twelve years old, with profound needs including assistance with eating, changing his diapers, and around-the-clock supervision.

I reminded the caller, "Our house is in boxes."

She explained, "I know, but we're desperate. He goes to court Tuesday morning, which will qualify him for a special-needs institution, but until then, he needs a home. The shelter is too much for him. He's been aggressive. He bit a child, so he's kicked out."

I caught TJ's eyes as he nodded sympathetically and replied, "We have plans we're obligated to this evening, but if you can't find anywhere else, you can bring him over in the morning."

TJ

When the case manager agreed to bring Phillip to our home, a part of me dreaded the impending reality of caring for a special-needs child. I felt unprepared to meet Phillip's needs and concerned we might make the situation worse. We had not spent much time with autistic children, so the lack of familiarity, his aggressive behavior, and our packed house built a lot of anxiety in me.

Prior to our certification, the state trained us on caring for children with emotional trauma, sexual abuse, physical abuse, neglect, developmental delays, and many other things. All foster parents receive similar training prior to their certification in their respective states. This training, while long and sometimes boring, helped prepare us for most of the children we welcomed into our home. Usually, when children with significant needs like Phillip's come into care, they are placed into therapeutic foster homes who have received advanced training to adequately meet the child's needs. In this situation, as the case manager made clear, there were no other options.

Jenn

Phillip pretty much crashed through the door into our house. While we remained on the porch with the case manager, he had made a beeline for the fridge and ripped out eggs and other food in search of something delicious. Before I could finish signing the custody papers, he sat on the carpet floor double-fisting Frosted Flakes. TJ and I met eyes, grinned, and chuckled in that no-turning-back-now kind of way.

TJ took Phillip outside to play so I could clean up the kitchen. From the kitchen window, I saw Phillip with his pants down around his ankles, shuffling away from TJ, who was still holding a football wondering what just happened. Evidently, Phillip didn't like to wear pants. Thankfully, we had built a fence around the backyard tall enough for a Great Dane. Privacy fence took on a new meaning.

Once they got back inside, I brought Phillip to the bathroom because we thought that maybe he took off his pants to communicate his need to use the toilet. At twenty-two years old and with no training in special education, I definitely had never changed the diaper of a twelve-year-old boy, but we figured it out.

While doing so, I noticed his entire legs and feet had dried to the point of cracking. I brought out lotion and ensured that he approved of my putting it on him. He responded like a purring kitten. This semi-grown, quiet boy was precious.

The next few days (seriously, days), I learned my role was to cuddle with him, put on lotion, massage his back, feed him—and nothing else. His hunger for affection proved how he needed loving touch so much, and, as I provided it, I wondered if he knew about his parents. It brought me tears of sadness at his circumstances and also tears of honor that God would choose me to love on him.

Once we realized Phillip would not let me have a minute without him in my arms, TJ took over the full care of Harmony during her last couple days with us. Then he took night duty with Phillip. Trying to keep Phillip lying in bed was like catching a duck. And the moment we thought he settled down to sleep, he jumped up and pulled on the blinds to see out the window. I heard TJ most of the night coaching, singing, and reassuring Phillip.

Contrary to first impressions, the timing of Phillip's stay worked really well. A house in boxes protected Phillip, the stuff, and us from his erratic movements. Since TJ was finished with duties at work because of our move, he could parent full-time with me. Phillip's arrival brought my life as I knew it to a complete halt, but the forced rest before a move helped me process all the life changes coming. In my three days with Phillip, I developed such empathy for parents with special-needs children; it led me toward working to provide relief care for special-needs families at a future duty station.

Phillip contained so much life and energy, even if he couldn't express it verbally. His dancing eyes and snuggles were worth missing the last goodbyes in the community we left. Looking back, we believe Phillip's time in our home was a gift sent from God.

TJ

Phillip left our home in the morning, and we departed for the airport that afternoon. After a week's vacation, we loaded up everything from our house and moved to another state. Even though we knew our time at this new duty station would be short, we decided to complete the certification process in this state, partially because they recognized our experience and training from the previous state. This is not always the case, but we appreciated the state's willingness to recognize the training we had already received.

After a couple other moves, we again ended up in a location where we planned to reside for more than a year. Even though my new responsibilities required me to travel a lot, we again decided to certify as foster parents. Our family had consisted of just Jenn and me for the last eighteen months, so we both felt a little apprehensive about expanding our family again. We have had the unique opportunity to go from having no children to having children and back again numerous times. Each time we welcome children into our family, I'm reminded of how much time parenting requires.

Takeaways

Phillip shifted our perspective of our life in the midst of community. The author of Hebrews writes, "Do not neglect to show hospitality to strangers, for thereby some have entertained angels unawares" (Hebrews 13:2). The verse implies a natural tendency to neglect strangers and also a devaluation of the spiritual weight hospitality carries. It is so much easier, and certainly more convenient, to quietly overlook the difficulties and troubles of those around us while we remain focused on accomplishing our goals or objectives. But, what

Chapter 6

Keeping Ashley Alive

"We make a living by what we get but make a life by what we give."

— **Sir Winston Churchill**[14]

TJ

As I held Ashley in the intensive care unit, I could hardly believe my eyes. Ashley was so small. Supporting her head with my fingers, her waist rested in the palm of my hand, and if I stretched out her legs, they reached only to the middle of my wrist. She looked even tinier wrapped in wires monitoring her heart rate and breathing. Even though the placement coordinator told us Ashley was born prematurely, we both expressed disbelief when we saw her for the first time. To this day,

I have yet to see a child as small as Ashley. Later, we took a photograph of her next to a ballpoint pen for a scale reference. After we brought Ashley home, when others asked her age, I answered, "She's negative four weeks," since she should have been in the womb for another month.

One of the first questions I asked the case manager in the ICU was, "What if she dies?" It was a legitimate question because of the medical miracle Ashley's mere survival represented. Ashley was not a healthy newborn baby, and now we were asked to care for this incredibly fragile life. I wanted to make sure everyone understood the gravity of the situation, and I also sought reassurance from the case manager that we would have adequate support to care for Ashley.

Jenn

I found TJ's question slightly unnerving and wondered if this story would have a happy ending. Ashley was born ten weeks premature to a drug-addicted mother. Machines and around-the-clock care had kept her alive for the last five weeks. Unlike our previous calls for foster children which started with the urgency of, "The children are in the office waiting for a home tonight" and ended with our rushing to prepare for their same-day arrival, we had time to weigh the decision with Ashley. Hospital staff knew her condition would necessitate at least another week in the hospital. We offered to consider caring for Ashley, so we met her, the nurse, and the case manager at the hospital for training.

TJ and I weren't alone in this decision. Six months beforehand, Jack, who just turned thirteen, and his fifth-grade sister Ariel had moved in with us. We called a family meeting. We needed everyone on board for this case to succeed. Jack and Ariel plopped on the couch after we beckoned them into the living room from their rooms.

Jack and Ariel blended well into our home, bringing life and personality, especially now that they were on summer break from school in a neighborhood full of kids. As such, our household operated in a relaxed state. We played cards, and Ariel worked on a reenactment of Tangled with friends. I became the host of what seemed like daily eating competitions for all the growing bodies around, hungry from riding bikes or swimming. TJ and I set aside Fridays for movie and popcorn night, all too often followed by dancing to video games.

TJ told them the decision to bring Ashley into our home would change our world. Beach days would be postponed; the Six Flags trip would be canceled; and the kids would have to pick up my slack in household chores. Jack and Ariel showed clear enthusiasm—I still picture their lit-up faces. They saw a chance to help do something cool and unique. Jack exclaimed, "This is even better than taking in the kitten!" which he spotted orphaned on the drive to summer camp and we had brought home a few weeks prior.

TJ and I carefully considered the weight of responsibility to simply keep Ashley alive. We were hesitant but also optimistic. Our family felt like a sports team about to take the field for a big game—a little anxious of the challenge to come, but full of excitement and hope. I pulled some of the little clothes and items I kept from Harmony out of the attic and smiled holding the itsy-bitsy pajamas.

After a nurse at the hospital gave us a crash course related to Ashley's required medical procedures, Ashley came home to us—all four pounds of her. On the day of departure from the special nursery, her nurse shared with me, "Ashley isn't quite ready to leave the hospital, but the staff needs a barrier to keep the parents from coming in. Last week, the boyfriend came in here and pulled a nurse's ponytail! We only send a baby home from this unit who is still receiving caffeine, maybe one in three hundred cases." As if I weren't nervous enough, this statement caused my eyes to go wide, and second thoughts crept into my mind.

Multiple times each night, our hearts stopped as TJ or I jumped out of bed to tend to her when the monitor said she stopped breathing. It sounded like a smoke alarm, jolting both her and us from deep sleep. Most of the time, the alarm's warning reflected an inability of the monitors to register her tiny movements, even though they were strapped on tight. But when her doctor kept seeing data that reflected poor breathing, he refused to take her off the machine. No one wants responsibility for assuming this sort of risk. Throughout the day, I added the prescribed caffeine to her milk to keep her awake or in a light enough sleep she would continue to breathe.

TJ

Caring for Ashley exhausted us. For the first month or so, Ashley slept in our room, and we listened through the night for her breathing. Our poor sleep was frequently interrupted with anxiety or alarm bells. As we became more accustomed to trusting the alarm, we moved Ashley to her own bedroom a half-flight of stairs immediately outside our bedroom. We kept both doors open and could react to her alarm in five to ten seconds if it went off.

A normal night would consist of Ashley going to bed before anyone else, and then, as she fell asleep, her heart rate slowed, so the monitor started beeping to alert us to go check on her. We would walk up the stairs, see her chest rising and falling, and then try and reposition the sensors on her body to better sense her breathing. This cycle would repeat sometimes as often as every five minutes, and sometimes we could go the full seventy minutes before she awoke crying for her bottle.

It was not always a calm process. You know how sometimes you wake up from a deep, deep sleep, sit up quick, and wonder where you are, or what time it is? Well, about every other night, one of us would wake up to Ashley's alarm in this sort of daze. We sprang upright in bed and wondered, "How long has it been going off?" After racing upstairs, I would find Ashley either asleep (and I'd watch and listen to see she breathed well) or moving in annoyance at the loud noise. Sometimes, I found Jenn up there trying to adjust the sensors, as I, in my haste, didn't check to see if she was still in bed or not. Fortunately, we never had an instance where Ashley stopped breathing, or if she did, the alarm's going off jarred her back awake and breathing before we noticed.

My wife handled it all with love and grace. She is an amazing woman with an incredibly high capacity level. Even though she spent many more nights awake and days homebound with Ashley than I did, the experience helped me recognize the work and sacrifice involved in caring for children with medical needs.

Jenn

Somehow, we found our new normal. Ashley didn't grow into newborn-sized pajamas for another month. Jack and Ariel were champs throughout. I have no idea how TJ kept his mind functioning at work all day. Members of our church lovingly brought meals, supplies, and even new games for Jack and Ariel.

A woman at church who worked as a neonatal nurse offered to babysit Ashley for an afternoon so the rest of us could go to the beach. I felt such a sense of freedom playing at the ocean: wrestling waves, soaking in the sun, burying Jack in the sand. Respite well-deserved, if I do say so myself. I can't remember Jack or Ariel complaining all summer, despite my exhausted parenting. They adored Ashley, as did many of our neighborhood friends. Simple summer staples like sprinklers and popsicles kept them happy, too.

We even hosted a teenage foster boy, Tom, for two weeks so that he could attend a special animation summer camp in town. I committed to this before we brought in Ashley. I felt as long as a transportation worker could bring him to and from camp, we could still host him with joy. I'm glad we did. He and Jack connected and kept up a friendship thereafter. We even had the privilege of watching Tom meeting his now-adoptive mom for the first time.

Don't let me fool you into patting me on the back as if I took this all in stride. I recall a particularly intense moment of madness, after about the billionth sleepless hour with Ashley's stupid monitor providing a tornado warning for the whole neighborhood. I felt stretched like a drum and thought in prayer, "I'm like a circus juggler with a dozen plates that keep crashing instead of spinning. Something has to stop. But what? It seems like You want each child, activity, and commitment to stay."

The responsibility felt heavy. From a macro-perspective, Jack, Ariel, and Ashley all grew and lived safely. In the micro day-to-day, it looked messy. The kids argued like hyenas, lost summer reading into the great abyss, stashed food like squirrels hiding acorns, and avoided showering like cats. I couldn't figure out why they avoided showers when I craved opportunities to take one! They also eagerly awaited reuniting with mom and dad, so they acted anxious. Ashley stayed rather constantly in my arms or a doctor's. We kept up multiple weekly community responsibilities. TJ had just returned from combat before the summer, and we knew he'd leave again within the month.

My frazzled hair and slight body odor must've cued a friend to bring over a good book. God used this book, Kisses from Katie by Katie Davis, to speak to me about a lie that was making me feel down. The lie was "God won't give you more than you can handle." I had more than I could handle.

God led me into a mess to show me His control—to prove He is the source of power, of love, and of a sound mind (2 Timothy 1:7). He used my overwhelmed state to bring me to maturity, dependence, and intimacy with Himself. God proved faithful in day-to-day grace, and He helped me grow so I could "handle" what I previously could not. Through an incremental "left foot forward in faith, right foot forward in deeds," God worked.

Living beyond what I could manage took faith. I wanted to operate under conditions I felt I could handle. Moving forward in foster parenting, saying yes, and continuing to parent humbled me and strengthened my faith. I found the day-to-day decisions to love, learn, and lean on God's sovereignty exercised my faith. All of this internal wrestling allowed the kids to experience the most lighthearted days with love. Additionally, we found children go about their days forgiving our faults with ease. They do not expect us to be perfect.

And even if we try to "make it perfect," often situations are out of our control.

For many reasons, we looked into a private school option for Jack and Ariel. We felt it was best for their situation. In discussions with the headmaster, we found provisions for a full scholarship for them both starting in the fall, not only while they remained in foster care but also after they returned to their parents. To us, this seemed like a great opportunity. So when the case manager shot it down immediately, I became reasonably frustrated.

After a bit of back and forth, one supervisor laid it out to me as if it should be as obvious as singing the alphabet song. She shared with me, "Sure, tuition is paid for, but once they go back to mom, she won't be able to drive them to school, and the school doesn't have buses. The children won't have free lunch, and the school lets out early. The kids won't have anywhere to go after school. The school places a lot of responsibility on parents, which their mom can't handle. In public school, they'll have a bus, breakfast, lunch, and free after-school care."

Oh. I hadn't thought about all that. I still disagree with the lack of attention paid to their education in any of the consideration. However, I realized my blindness to barriers related to poverty. I wanted their best, but my perceived version of their best wasn't actually best.

As for Ashley's case, I felt anxious because the case manager kept changing. As a result, the state couldn't keep track of information, which was especially important with her medical needs. The case manager set up her Medicaid wrong so we received bills from her eye doctor, and each week a different driver came to pick her up for her birth mother visitation, each one seemingly surprised and unprepared to handle her medical equipment. I had to coach each driver on what to do when the alarm sounded as she drove. Ashley's mom felt anxious by all of this, too. She certainly had a legitimate reason for her frustration, especially when case managers would not return her calls, didn't notify her of important meetings, or failed to schedule visits at times convenient for her.

TJ

When states remove children from their birth parents and place them into foster care, most parents begin a process to regain custody of their children. Case managers assigned to families build a "case plan" or checklist for parents, which include education and assistance to help bring their kids back under their care. Housing, food stamps, parenting classes, rehab, job training, counseling, support groups—you name it, parents have access to it. As long as they work toward completing the plan, they stay on the path of reuniting with their child.

However, birth parents' progress often depends on one point of contact: the case manager. Case managers have a lot to handle with the children's side of the case, in addition to referring parents to treatment and scheduling their appointments or visitations. Many case managers handle between fifteen and forty cases composed of at least one child and his/her entire family network. This single person serves as the coach, investigator, trainer, safety-net, advocate, prosecutor, listening ear, assistant—so many roles. For birth parents, foster parents, family members, and children, the case managers hold shaky circumstances together like glue.

Jenn

When Ashley's mom couldn't reach a case manager, she rightfully felt concerned. She became insecure. "Does the case manager not like me?" she wondered. For almost a month, no one managed the case. I worried too, knowing that everything may fall apart without the consistency a stable case manager provides. When her baby came into care, the mom felt exposed and hurt. She did not expect to lose the baby she'd carried for months, and no one walked her through the traumatic circumstances.

I wrote encouraging notes and shared our support of her whenever we met. By my caring for her daughter and sending notes, calling to check in, or giving her rides home from visits, we built trust. I also firmly communicated, "I am not trying to adopt your daughter. I hope you are able to pull your life together and be a great mom for her, if that's what you want. I'm cheering for you, not against you." This message may seem obvious and unnecessary to communicate, but we found that communicating our hope for the families' restoration provided reassurance to the birth parents and helped keep our emotions under control.

Ashley's mom felt thankful and loved because I cared for her daughter, and I hoped for her success as a mother. If foster parents communicate both of these messages, we create an opportunity to help others in the midst of their pain and broken life. Naturally, Ashley's mom started calling me for encouragement just as she would a friend. She asked questions; I prayed with her when she was down and brought Ashley to meet her dying grandpa.

When a new case manager stopped in for the four-month check-in, and indifferently notified me, "Once Ashley is physically stable, she will move to a relative who will adopt her. We're going to add another visitation to Ashley's weekly schedule for the aunt to spend time with her." I felt blood rush through my body. This is the part where emotions want to take control and make me scream (on the inside), "You're not taking my baby!" The case manager patiently answered my badgering questions. She assured me this move provided long-term kinship care for Ashley.

While moving to live with the aunt who cared for her brother offered permanency and was technically good news, I felt so bummed. I wondered about her mother and if this case manager knew what she was doing. When I sat to reflect, I realized that, without conscious intention, I had dreamt about raising Ashley forever. For the next couple weeks, I wrestled with distrust of the case manager and envy of this family member, receiving a soon-to-be healthy little baby girl who felt like my baby girl. I felt justified: "I've been the one laboring through these hard, endless hours tending to her needs, keeping her alive, and bonding. I'm finally seeing her smile!" The only other woman I wanted raising her was Ashley's birth mom. I spoke on the phone with the aunt and watched her care for Ashley at a couple visitations, which provided me with ease and confidence in her. A stranger is scary, but love builds with just a few interactions.

TJ

That fall, I prepared for a long work trip, and I suspected that by the time I returned, Ashley would be gone. After learning about her aunt, I believed my kiss on her forehead before flying away would be the last one I ever gave her. I love Ashley and still smile writing about her.

The state nearly always prefers foster children to live with family members as opposed to non-related foster parents. Ashley stayed with us for less than six months, but even if she had been with us as a foster child for years, this aunt she'd never met had legal deference to raise her. Although Ashley's birth parents cannot raise her, if the child remains in the same family, one less piece of her life is broken. And who knows? Maybe one day her mother will rehabilitate and play an active role in her life. This ranking of family preference is a somewhat difficult fact to accept in some cases, but it is important to recognize when one signs up to participate as foster parents.

In our marriage, I felt I was the one to keep this fact in front of us. When we fell in love with a child, we naturally imagined our future with that child and want to adopt him or her and parent them for life. In all of our cases, adoption was never a possibility for us, although we agreed to be adoptive parents, if needed, to many of the children. Only when the court decided birth parents and relatives could not care for the children would we have the opportunity to adopt. Plenty of foster parents have broken hearts over distant relatives popping up out of the blue years into a case, even after the state asked foster parents to consider and plan to adopt the children but before court proceedings made it final.

However, thousands of families do adopt from foster care, and over one hundred thousand children living in foster care currently seek adoptive families.[15] In our case, unless we specifically stated we only wanted to care for children seeking an adoptive family, the children placed in our home would hopefully return to parents or family. To adopt children from foster care usually means they've spent months in someone else's foster home, and, for some reason, the current foster parents do not or cannot adopt.

Jenn

The day arrived for Ashley to move about a month after TJ left. I spent the morning writing notes to her aunt detailing Ashley's daily routine and fishing out tiny onesies from the mound of clean laundry to pack in her bags. I helped load Ashley and her belongings in her new family's vehicle. After I buckled up Ashley in her car seat, I kissed her on the forehead, stuck my pinky in her hand to grasp for the last time, and then the family drove away.

I sighed as my understanding of the finality of the situation hit me, but I then quickly realized Ariel had bolted inside moments before. Ariel had three neighborhood girlfriends over playing, and I didn't anticipate how upset she would be. Chills ran through me as I realized she just lost the only sister she'd ever had. Ariel knew Ashley would be moving, but she was not prepared emotionally. Her friends rushed to Ariel's bed to comfort her, and I joined in, too.

We embraced while Ariel cried, and, through her grief, I became aware of and silently thanked God for the peace He'd given me so I could even comfort Ariel. I had used the previous month to process through my feelings about Ashley's going and God's good plans for her. By the time she left, I knew I would miss her, but I also felt confident with the "rightness" of the move. I should have helped the kids prepare for the transition and use the situation to help illustrate how God can comfort us in moments of intense grief. It caused me to wonder how often I fail to recognize the power, peace, and grace God provides for those who trust in Him.

Even after Ashley left our care, her mom and I continued to write and talk, but then she kind of faded away. As foster parents, we always expected to nurture, love, and comfort children. We didn't realize it would include adults as well. God used our relationships with children to provide a context where faith could be displayed. By loving Ashley in a way that honored her mom, we got to love her, too.

Takeaways

Interacting with the various adults and government services involved in children's cases also drained us far more than any of the children's' behavior ever did. What should be a simple task takes way too much time and paperwork. That constant inconvenience compounded with ideological differences steals energy.

Sometimes foster parenting felt like rainbows and butterflies; the storm had passed, and life was beautiful and calm. Other times, it felt like trying to walk with your foot caught in a bear trap; you're frustrated at the inability to do something simple, and it's really painful.

Technically, the state holds custody of foster children while foster parents are their legal guardians. However, the birth parents still have legal rights. It's confusing. This "trinity" of parenting is one distinguishing difference between fostering and adopting. All three parties must work with one another.

Foster parents have freedom over most day-to-day living decisions to guide a child's development. The state provides oversight, insurance, financial support, education, and the final say on all matters. Birth parents have input with decisions and, of course, they contribute to the nurturing and development of the children as well.

Despite the stress, we think Ashley's case represents another success, even though we miss her terribly. We agree with philosopher Andrew Bernstein when he says, "Remember that stress doesn't come from what's going on in your life. It comes from your thoughts about what's going on in your life."[16]

Ashley's case caused us to reflect upon a lot of things. Exhaustion will do that.

We compared our faith in technology and medicine to our faith in God. Frequently, we placed our dependence and trust in her breathing monitor. As long as it was attached and operating, we assumed Ashley was all right. We became accustomed to the monitor's presence. Then, when we took her off of the monitor, for any length of time whatsoever, even for a bath, our nerves quickened, and we constantly attended to her. Part of our nervousness came from her being another person's child whom the state had entrusted to us.

Regardless of the reason, we felt convicted about our lack of reliance on God—not that we should feel guilty about trusting the monitor. We found that we lacked the same dependency and expectations of prayer that we had placed upon this monitor. It was so easy to place our trust in this man-made device, which, more often than not, gave us wrong signals. But we were not as vigilant in keeping her uplifted in prayer or as confident in prayer's effectiveness.

God's love never fails, and He loves us more than we can comprehend. But how quick we are to think some things are beyond His control! While we firmly believe in using medical technology to help prevent death or heal sickness, we know prayer is a wonderful complement to whatever medical treatment doctors prescribe. Looking back, we should have prayed for Ashley with the same diligence we had in keeping her monitor attached and with the same faith in the result.

Chapter 7

Winning the Daily-Double

"Only those who will risk going too far can possibly find out how far they can go."

—T.S. Eliot[17]

Jenn

When TJ and I purchased our second home, we considered how the layout would maximize future placements: everything from having a good bathtub and big rooms, to a bonus room upstairs separate from the other bedrooms and near ours to prevent undesirable evening activities like running away. We sought out a safe street with a big backyard. Accommodating these desires within our budget meant selecting a house that required major renovations and other updates. We constructed a bonus room out of attic space over the garage and committed it to God to "use it how You see fit." We furnished the space with two twin beds and one of my dressers from grade school.

Soon the summer break with Jack, Ariel, and Ashley came to a close. I attended school orientation with the kids (which, by the way, is totally awkward for a twenty-five-year-old mom of two middle school kids. You'd think I was naked with how many mamas looked me up and down.). As we adjusted to middle school life, we all agreed we could care for another foster child if needed. I began praying for a larger vehicle, and within a day I had a Facebook message from a friend's mother halfway across the country asking if we could use a van. (Wow!)

The day after we picked up the van, in the midst of afternoon homework help, I took a call from the foster care agency. By now I've memorized most social workers' phone extensions, so I usually know if it's a placement worker when I answer the phone. "Good afternoon, Mr. Johnson."

Mr. Johnson: "Hi! I hope all is well. Hey, listen, we have a three and a four year old that need a home. Are you interested?"

Me: "You know I have two teenagers and Ashley's still on the monitor, right?"

Mr. Johnson: "Yes."

Me: "I'll call TJ and ask, but keep calling around and try to find a home for them. What do you know about them?"

Mr. Johnson: "One was discharged from the hospital today after falling out of a two-story window. They're at the office now. I don't know much. I only have one other house I can call, so I'll probably be calling you back."

Me: "All right, well, I'll call TJ."

Click.

Ring-ring at TJ's work.

Me: "Can I speak with Captain Menn, please?"

TJ, clearly needing to be somewhere quick, rushed me along: "What's up?"

Me: "We got a call for a four and three year old. They don't have much info but need a place tonight."

TJ: "Sure, we already prayed about possibly taking more kids, so I'm good with it if you are. Either way, I gotta go. Love you." Click.

I sat an extra few seconds in silence, not expecting him to decide so quickly. I think if I would've asked what he wanted on his pizza tonight, it would've taken longer to decide. I was also in shock of the pending reality. "I am about to have five kids. Five kids, ages 13, 11, 4, 3, and 12 weeks." Or maybe I was just thinking slowly from sleepless nights.

I shared the news with Jack and Ariel, excused myself from homework help by providing more snacks, and went upstairs to move Ashley's crib back down into our bedroom. Previous experience told me to keep the new little kids in a bedroom together, so Jack's and Ariel's lives were disturbed as little as necessary. Plus, I knew the little ones would want to comfort one another.

By 6:00 p.m., Jasmine and Darius stood nervously in our living room, peeking out from behind the investigator with wide eyes. I tried to draw them out to play with a couple toys while TJ signed papers. They came with a grocery bag of belongings and remained silent as we ate and prepared for bed.

I learned by mid-morning the next day that their silence was less from fear and had more to do with their inability to speak coherent words. And so I began the standard two-week chaos of having a new professional stopping by every other day, and a new handful of appointments for each child. It felt like the first placement all over again: three little ones with the baby requiring special medical attention. This time, we had Jack and Ariel, too, but thankfully I knew exponentially more about parenting.

TJ

Within a few weeks, we drove the three little ones on a fourteen-hour road trip to New York to interview for a position as an instructor at the United States Military Academy at West Point in the Social Sciences Department. We also used the trip as a type of pre-deployment getaway. Unfortunately, Jack and Ariel stayed behind because their parents would not let them leave the state.

The Department of Children Services certified a couple of our friends to stay in our home and watch the kids while we took the trip. Other friends welcomed us to stay with them while we were at West Point. Friends like these are phenomenal. We prepared what we could, and God provided for the needs we couldn't prepare for. Even though everyone was disappointed the big kids couldn't come with us, the separation gave Jack and Ariel some quiet time away from the little ones and a break from us, too.

Though we could barely stuff three car seats into our sedan, Jasmine and Darius seemed quite content on the drive. They rarely left a single room their whole life, so seeing water, bridges, and changing scenery amazed them. Having grown up on a farm, I really enjoy scenic drives and sometimes get a little excited when viewing beautiful landscapes or interesting farming operations. About halfway to New York, the kids had already picked up a new phrase, "Whoa! Look at that!" after hearing me repeat it a few dozen times.

Similar to the beach trip with Shelly and Holly, this trip provided an opportunity to bond with the children. We enjoyed showing the kids around West Point, playing at different playgrounds, and telling them stories from our college days there. It also gave Jenn and me lots of time to learn some of their mannerisms. While awake and gazing, they constantly rocked themselves back and forth, jamming out to an internal rhythm. When sleeping, you could hear Jasmine sucking her middle finger, like an infant. Darius stuttered when he was excited and tried to communicate the reason for his exuberance. Even though we initially hesitated taking the young ones with us, I'm really glad we did. The adventurous nature of a road trip and uninterrupted time in the car helped solidify our new family.

A few days after we returned home, I deployed.

Jenn

Parenting a wide array of ages by myself challenged me to say the least. An infant, preschoolers, and teens all have such different needs. Even if the baby blissfully slept past 6:00 a.m., I needed to be up waking kids, packing lunches, gathering homework, and sending them to catch the bus.

By the time the preschoolers went down at night, the teens were eager to talk uninterrupted by little ones. Ashley's routine kept me sanely chugging through the day and night: sleep, wake, eat, change diaper, play, repeat. Oh, I can't forget to mention the beeeeeeeeeeeep beeeeeeeeeeeeep beeeeeeeeep from her monitor.

Driving to kids' therapy multiple times a week and managing the information streaming in from three different sets of case managers filled the gaps. Each case had its own case manager, lawyer or advocate, birth parents, social worker, and therapeutic professionals. Medical staff came weekly to download information from Ashley's monitor, and she also had weekly pediatric or specialist appointments.

Sometimes, we felt isolated because of the behaviors and daily challenges we faced but could not share. Explaining special needs to the public proves difficult to articulate and often would have violated confidentiality requirements anyway. The kids' speech therapists, occupational therapists, and behavioral specialists seemed to understand our experience. Not only did they get it, but they helped in amazing ways!

And, of course, this season happened to coincide with launching a ministry to recruit foster parents, hosting a dozen middle schoolers on a church retreat, and Ariel's birthday extravaganza. I even showered, sometimes. My favorite time of day was when Jack and Ariel came home from school, and everyone happily snacked and played together. Neighbor kids or my friends sometimes joined in, too.

With every case we recognized the support of community, but during this time our church was a life-line. Individuals mowed our yard and washed our windows. They brought us meals or gift cards. They donated electrician and plumbing labor. They offered professional counseling services, prayer, house cleaning, games or toys, furniture, friendship, and babysitting. We felt encouraged that we were not alone in this endeavor.

Once the case manager scheduled Ashley's move, I received a call from Jasmine and Darius's social worker. "We've been looking for another home for Jasmine and Darius, but we heard you have a spot for their sister now," she said.

Me: "Excuse me? I'm not sure I know what you're talking about."

Social worker: "Tamika, their sister. She's, uh, fifteen months old. We need for them to be together. If you won't take her, just say so."

Me: "I'm sorry. This is the first I'm hearing about Tamika."

Social worker: "Oh, nobody probably told you about her because you wouldn't be able to take her anyway with the other baby girl you had. Well, will you take her? Otherwise, we'll keep looking somewhere for the kids."

Me: "Oh, I understand now. Ashley is still with us. She's not moving for a few weeks, so let me check with my husband, but we should be able to take Tamika once Ashley goes."

Yikes! Did I just say that?

Everyone seemed eager to reunite the siblings. The state made it sound urgent. Jack and Ariel lacked the excitement from the summer's choice about Ashley, but they agreed this little sister needed to be with her siblings. I waited to tell Jasmine and Darius until I knew when she would come.

Once Ashley left, Tamika's arrival date was postponed a month. All the rush screeched to a halt because the social worker couldn't pencil in time to pick her up at one home and bring her over to ours. Both Tamika's foster mom at the time and I thought it was ridiculous for these kids to wait for that reason. We offered to arrange the transfer independently, to no avail. Eventually, our persistence and clamoring resulted in Tamika's arrival just before Thanksgiving.

During this waiting period, I wrote several emails to TJ overseas.

TJ,

...Okay so you're probably going to think I'm...well, I was going to say crazy, but I don't think you will...I'm being me.

What about putting in a request to Mr. Johnson at Children Services for a 3-6th-grade girl that could share a room with Ariel? Now that she's in the bunkbed room, it got me thinking about it, as well as seeing how social she was when hosting the retreat. I think it would be energizing for her (and character building, I'm sure, too). I asked her about it tonight, just to get a feel for what her first reaction was and she got really excited and she chattered about...

"I want her to be just like me...no wait then we'd fight like Katy and Kelly. I want her to be the opposite of me."

My reply: "Then she'd want pink all over and play rap music"

Ariel: "AHHH, no. She'd just have to get used to my country music (with an attitude)...or I can put it on my headphones." Then, all excited, she's like, "Please! Tell TJ I want one. A sister. Not like a little sister, like a fun sister."

So, it's on her Christmas list. Mine, too. Just think. Some little girl is going to be alone in a shelter on Christmas...

OK, those are my important things. Have fun replying.
—Jenny
P.S. Ariel also got excited at the thought of driving a church van around.

Two days later TJ replied,

Jenny,

No, absolutely not, as to another child in the home beside Tamika. At least not for a month.

Tonight was a long night, and just the beginning of many.

I love you and am going to go to bed.

—TJ

I dropped it. No more talk of another girl. And within a couple days I wrote,

Subject: And then there were five again!
TJ,

I'm excited. Tamika is cute, and quiet, and asleep. Jasmine is thrilled. THRILLED. She's got her big sister voice and attitude back. It's so cute, and she dressed dolls in Tamika's clothes for a long time. Darius is ecstatic too. He kissed her on the cheek a million times.
Lovin' it
—Jenny

The kids and I took a four-hour road trip to my parents' house to celebrate Thanksgiving. By now, Jack and Ariel had developed a special friendship and routine with my family, so they were excited to travel for the holiday. My parents and my brother who still live in the local area loved on the kids unbelievably well. Walking in the front door and being greeted with my parents' and siblings' hugs felt like taking a heavy backpack off, especially when I visited during TJ's deployments. The kid-to-adult ratio shifted completely, and I left behind chores. Jack and my brother spent hours playing video games while my dad set up a tent in the living room for the kids to play in. I could feel our love tanks filling up.

Like most holidays, the visit ended with lots of hugs and wishing we could stay longer. We all piled back into the van for the trip home. The day after returning, I received a phone call from my neighbor Stacy, frantic about her teenage daughter Hannah.

"Jenn, Hannah just ran away. She's walking down Deere Street and won't get in the car. We had a fight about her dad."

"OK, I'll go get her," I answered. I loaded up the little kids (Jack and Ariel were at a friend's house), and we hit the road. When we got down the road, I rolled down the window and hollered: "Hey, want a ride, pretty lady?"

Hannah frowned and shook in tears. "I don't want to go home."

I told her, "You're not. Let's go eat pizza at my place and then go with me to Target for some stuff."

Hannah stayed the night, shared her conflict, and determined not to go home until she resolved it. So we added Hannah to our family mix. Her parents said they felt peace knowing she was safe, and I could keep them updated.

TJ

Foster parenting brings about a reliance on the community more than we ever anticipated. Our parents, family members, neighbors, church, and the children's professional services staff all helped us along the way. It was neat to see God provide and to experience these blessings.

Our families provided incredible support to us during our time as foster parents. When we traveled to Jenn's parents', the kids were bounding out of the van yelling for grandpa and grandma before I could even get the baby out of the car seat. On more than one occasion, my family flew in to visit or watch the kids when we needed a babysitter for an extended period of time. Especially during my deployments, family support kept Jenn sane.

Our friends from church also helped a lot, whether it meant picking up the children from appointments, babysitting while Jenn ran an errand, or consistently encouraging us. It is difficult to convey the impact our friends made not only on our ability to foster but also on the lives of the children in our home. Without the support of friends and family, I know our experience would have been dramatically different.

Of course, our neighbors also played a role, and none of them spent more time at our house than Hannah's family. We had spent a lot of time with Hannah's family before she arrived in our home. Stacy and Jenn walked together in the mornings, and when Stacy started training for a marathon, I occasionally joined her on my morning runs. Our families prepared meals for each other, watched recitals, and attended church together. Jenn and Stacy exchanged keys to each other's places and chatted about day-to-day life. Ariel often walked down to visit with Hannah's grandma and play with the dogs.

When Stacy called and Jenn brought Hannah home, she had no doubt I would be on board despite our previous email exchange. Hannah faced a difficult time in her life and God used us to keep her in a safe environment, close to her family.

Jenn

When Stacy called about Hannah, I didn't connect the situation at all to Ariel's desire for a foster sister. I knew Hannah, and considered her a friend. Her mom Stacy is the type of neighbor who brought over chicken soup when we first moved in and watched the kids when we clearly needed a night out.

God had prepared us for taking on another child but not in the way we thought He would. When I felt like bringing in another teenage girl, TJ shot the idea down. OK, he's at war and busy, I reasoned. I didn't want to add to his stress by being a wife-gone-wild on the homefront.

Then Hannah came. Once she decided to stay a while, we set her up in Ariel's bunk bed. As I saw them interact more, I realized Ariel got her Christmas wish early. God had definitely prepared us for Hannah. Her presence gave Ariel an older sister-roommate to laugh with and the companionship I needed during a deployment when I felt exhausted in the evenings. Her assistance with the little kids was invaluable, especially during the busy holiday season.

I wouldn't have defined it as "foster parenting." She came without the drain of social worker opinions, interventions, and court drama. I empathized with her situation because I had already been journeying it with her family. I knew the complex situation, so I gave her space to grieve the conflicts happening. My personal response to Hannah also triggered a greater empathy for the other children in our home. It renewed my patience for their behavior.

Hannah ended up staying with us about six weeks, which was just enough time to help mend her relationship with her parents, let TJ come home to two new beautiful girls (Tamika and Hannah!), share Christmas with our bountiful crew, bring Ariel to the realization that sharing a room isn't "da-bomb 4life," and further bond Hannah's family to ours.

TJ

Even though we can look back with fond memories now, this time was pretty taxing. While deployed, I specifically remember a few phone calls which ended with Jenn sobbing and telling me she just needed me home. I usually tried to call her at the end of my work shift, which happened to coincide with her bedtime. Of course, that is when she was already tired, which probably didn't help matters much.

I also called Jenn at the end of my day because the inability to assist my wife when she needed me most bothered me. If I called her at the beginning of the day, her problems or difficulties consumed many of my thoughts. Calling her at the end of the day allowed me to remain mentally focused on the missions at hand. The last thing she needed to deal with was a husband who died in a helicopter crash because he was distracted by events at home while flying a mission overseas.

After those phone calls I did the only thing I really could do to help her in our current situation—I prayed. I prayed a lot and trusted the Lord would answer my prayers. Desperation effectively drives us to prayer. Shamefully, I admit I pray for Jenn more when I know she hurts than I do when things are going well. This season tested and strengthened our relationship with each other and with the Lord.

Takeaways

There's always a good reason to say "no" to a placement. Adding more children into the mix may seem crazy, or we think maybe the "timing just isn't right." The calls seemed to come when we hosted company, just returned from vacation, faced a deployment to war within the week, or dealt with other kids feeling sick.

And we knew what comes with a placement—not just the adjustment to parenting new children, but also visits from case managers and every assessment under the sun. Life keeps churning, too: friends come over, holiday parties beckon, Sunday school continues, ministry meetings and work still get done, even gardening and reading good books stay on our minds. Besides spending most waking hours at work, TJ applied to graduate schools and ran a marathon, while Jenn managed a counseling practice. Together, we completely remodeled our home.

The preschoolers attended speech and occupational therapy three times a week, they'd wake up baby Ashley, push the older kids' buttons, bolt from us in parking lots, and bite others. Jack hit puberty with accompanying mood swings.

We see and know the tradeoffs involved when we say "yes." Some people told us the season we lived in seemed like the perfect time to foster, before we had kids of our own. This might have been true, but our twenties were also the perfect time to travel, build a career, complete additional education, live in a city, and have lots of other non-kid-friendly adventures. As young parents, we had a steep learning curve.

We also thought it was one of the least convenient times to care for foster children. Why not wait to do it until we had a baby of our own and were in parent-mode already? Or why not wait until we had older children who were more self-sufficient and could help? Or take some time for ourselves first? Or wait until we raised kids right and knew what we'd be facing? Why not wait until we were out of the military and could settle somewhere? Why not wait until the children in our home returned to their parents before taking more?

Why? Because they're children, and their lives don't wait for our plans. Waiting for the perfect time to foster parent is like waiting for the ocean to stay still.

We all tend to sacrifice more for those we know and love. Familiarity helps us empathize. For example, in the midst of a busy week, if a family friend calls with someone in the hospital or broken down on the side of the road, we suddenly have time to help. If we are willing to sacrifice for those we know and love in crisis, we should be willing to take on more responsibility for all people whom God knows and loves. God is calling His followers to love and care for the neighbors we don't already know. He will bless our obedience.

During crazy seasons of flux, when circumstances threaten to overwhelm, we realized that,

God is able to make all grace abound to you, so that having all sufficiency in all things at all times, you may abound in every good work...He who supplies seed to the sower and bread for food will supply and multiply your seed for sowing and increase the harvest of your righteousness.

2 Corinthians 9:8-10 (ESV)

These words above provide an energizing promise. "Grace abounding" implies more than survival. It implies more than we need. When we committed to His service, He provided more than we needed. We found God gives grace to serve Him wholly and abundantly in the midst of any trial—even the comings and goings of children we adore, combat deployments, and the many loads of laundry in between.

Chapter 8

Biting, Lying, and Dirty Dancing

"[Parents need to] give and show love to a child all the time, even when her behavior is poor. Does this sound like permissiveness? It is not. Rather, it is doing first things first. A child's emotional tank must be filled before any effective training of discipline can take place. A child with a full love tank can respond to parental guidance without resentment."

—Gary Chapman[18]

Jenn

People frequently ask us, "How do you handle the baggage the children bring into your home?" First, we handle it by God's grace. Secondly, they don't have baggage; they have leaks.

If we stick with Dr. Chapman's analogy above, then foster children often have cracks and punctures in their love tanks from the way they've been treated. The children usually come from a world that thwarts their development. As a result, foster parents should probably handle attachment, discipline, and poor behavior differently than parents who have raised the children since birth. I spent most of my time filling emotional tanks. Figuring out the right adaptive response is like fixing a leak when you don't know where the crack is.

Several of our foster children entered our home without the simple concept of how to play. As a child, I carefully played for hours with an enormous, intricate doll house my dad had made me. I even tied dozens of bows on my frilly comforter. My dolls all had names and specific places to go.

In contrast, most of our young foster children tore stuff up. I found books ripped to shreds, decapitated dolls, and fuzz from the guts of stuffed animals almost daily. For example, while spending a weekend at my parents' house, Jasmine brought a destructive force comparable to a hurricane on that delicate doll house I had maintained so perfectly as a child. Ariel left her initials written or carved into just about everything, her dresser and closet walls included.

While sometimes this reckless behavior can be a way of acting out emotions, it is often a result of caregivers never teaching children how to play properly. Many foster children have had trash for toys or abandoned belongings time and time again as their parents loaded up the family to move at a moment's notice. Many of our children rarely spent time around kids who knew how to play before coming into foster care.

Some of our teenagers never had clothes in drawers, let alone places for toys. Living on a campground for years or sharing bedrooms with drug addicts and strangers rarely includes training on proper toy etiquette. So, yeah, finding ruined belongings, especially sentimental ones, is a bummer. At least it's just stuff.

When we stopped at a fast food play-place, Jasmine and Darius grabbed my leg in fear. It was just so foreign and big. I suppose when a tissue is your only toy to keep you content, a play-place is terrifying. Eventually, they happily played near it, but the inside of it might as well have been a tank of sharks. At a bouncy house, being near the small side tube that fills the castle with air was more than enough fun for these two.

In contrast, they likened going to the dentist with a holiday treat. Seriously, we counted down the days to dentist visits like Advent calendars for Christmas, and when the nurse called each name to go back for Xrays, their faces lit up with happiness. Even with sharp metal objects prying open their mouths, they grinned.

Going to the doctor was like offering them ice cream. Immunizations—the cherry on top. If one kid felt hurt or sick, the other faked an ailment for the sake of a Band-Aid. I'm pretty sure Darius at least once intentionally hurt himself for the sake of the attention. They loved adults caring for them because it was not normal. Any attention in their direction satisfied the constant hunger for love. Even uncomfortable attention was worth it.

So, you parents out there, take heart. Playing with your little kids makes a difference! It's key to all-around development. And, you parents whose children scream at needles and sharp metal objects approaching their face, good! They have security and know of much better ways to receive love. Keep it up.

Our home may have been Toy Story's worst nightmare, but at least going to the dentist brought smiles all around.

Helping develop a healthy worldview and emotional state is one reason why foster parenting can be so redemptive. Many children act as miniature versions of their birth parents. They witnessed dysfunctional behavior (at a minimum) and learned to live with dysfunction. When we modeled and instructed healthy, stable, living behavior, the children's attitudes and conduct changed accordingly. Children adapt through modeling and instruction. Some children seemed physically, emotionally, and spiritually healthy, and we encouraged their growth. Others were heading in a poor direction, and we helped change their trajectory.

As Christians, we thought a key component of our parenting involved providing a loving atmosphere to show children and their parents the love of Jesus Christ. His constant love and presence informed our parenting decisions. Jesus Christ led a sinless, holy life and sacrificed His life so He could take the blame for my sins and shortcomings. Then I can live a new life under the favor of God.

As a teenager, when I understood the relationship God wanted with me, my worldview, emotions, and behaviors changed significantly. I went from ashamed and identity-seeking to confident and seeking to love Him in return. Similarly, we observe foster children and their parents grow as they understand the worth they have to God. The transformation from disparity to hope or from anger to humility and kindness is a great joy to witness.

TJ

If you are a Christian interested in serving your community through foster parenting, you can rest assured that you do not have to hide your religious beliefs to participate. We led transparent and open conversations with the state's foster care workers about our faith and how it informed our decision-making. Case managers, home-study evaluators, judges, lawyers, professional advocates, birth parents, foster children, and other foster parents knew Christianity was more than a religious philosophy for us.

In no way did we need to hide our efforts to pray for the children or back away from sharing Jesus' message of grace and love with our foster children. At the same time, we never forced church attendance or other religious activities on children who were old enough to have their own informed opinion. We tried to emulate Jesus Christ. We shared His message of love and repentance, and we outlined His morals as guidelines for how to interact with one another.

On our refrigerator, we had a sheet of paper with the following principles as our values, and we included regular teachings on the reasoning behind them:

Principles of God
Principle 1:   Love the Lord.
Principle 2:   Rebellion against authority is rebellion against God.
Principle 3:   Personal responsibility.
Principle 4:   Work ethic.
Principle 5:   The Golden Rule: Treat others as you would want to be treated.
Principle 6:   Honor your mother and father.
Principle 7:   Your body is the temple of God.
Principle 8:   You reap what you sow.
Principle 9:   Guard your tongue.
Principle 10: The secret to success is to seek the Kingdom of God.[19]

The principles were less about house rules and more about defining how we operated. We tried to incorporate these principles into any disciplinary discussions we had with the children.

Jenn

Beyond these principles for the home, TJ and I tried to employ adaptive approaches to foster parenting. These children experienced tough emotions and situations, which produced maturity in them in some areas. However, other areas like speech, coordination, and life skills seemed stifled. Huge gaps in education sometimes existed. Delays in development or dysfunctional thinking in foster children led to unique situations where "normal parenting" fell short.

In one instance, we cared for middle school kids who missed complete years of elementary school, but restarted with their respective age classmates rather than picking up where they left off academically. In terms of age, educators labeled them as "middle school," but in other life skills and knowledge, they would have placed them much younger.

Sociologists describe this complicated development by comparing a child's chronological age to his functioning age. If a teenage boy functioned like a six year old with regard to process management and personal hygiene, then I had to adjust my expectations for his abilities and responses according to his six-year-old capacity, rather than what I expected from a teenager. On the flip side, he reasoned well and communicated like an adult from years of surviving independently. Tricky, tricky.

This type of parenting adjustment rarely came naturally to us. Behaviors startled us. I know, in theory, foster children differ from children raised in healthy families. But sometimes I forgot. Living with the effects of their maltreatment and learned behaviors brought both sobriety and stunned laughter at some of the unexpected actions.

TJ

Welcoming children into our family was not always smooth sailing. Adjusting to a new equilibrium in the home took time. Jenn is usually a much more easygoing person than I am. I suppose birth orders may have something to do with it (since I am a firstborn and she is a middle child), but our personality differences are even more pronounced in our parenting styles. I am typically a firm black-and-white disciplinarian, while Jenn applies more grace to situations.

Coming from an army-officer perspective probably didn't help me much either. You see, in the army, a pretty common line of thinking is to bring very high standards of discipline with you into the job, particularly when you take command or assume responsibility of soldiers. The reasoning for this approach lies in the fact that you can usually ease up on these standards as the men and women you work with become more familiar with your expectations and priorities.

On the other hand, if an officer moves into a new position of authority and overlooks misconduct or is reluctant to discipline soldiers, the members of that unit will adjust their conduct accordingly. Later, when the commander wants to enforce the previously overlooked rules, he or she will have a much harder time because the soldiers are accustomed to a certain level of discipline. To avoid seeming hypocritical, most leaders choose to set high expectations at the beginning and then practice individual cases of discretion when circumstances warrant it.

We found the exact opposite approach worked much better for most foster children. Thus, when children first arrived into our home, I made a conscious effort to avoid correcting minor behavioral flaws and focused on welcoming the children into our home. They needed to know we were there to protect and care for them, not scold or correct their every shortcoming.

Jenn and I both disciplined the children for more significant offenses such as hitting or fighting, but for the most part, the first two weeks the children were in our home, we tried to fill those love tanks Jenn mentioned before. Even though this went against my natural inclinations and my intuition as an army officer, we found this approach worked well. The children often arrived scared and very timid. Some little ones were afraid of my mere presence, and we really had no idea what kind of experiences were in their past, so we focused on loving them and helping establish expectations.

Jenn

When Jasmine and Darius first arrived, they jibber-jabbered like Charlie Brown's teacher. They came from a world (or room in a boarded-up house) of their own, with language and habits that followed. I'd say, "What do you want?" and Jasmine might parrot, "What do you want?" or Darius would confidently spurt out sounds with no meaning.

But then I started to understand a few things very clearly—for example, profanity, with such excellent context they'd impress rap stars. In the bath tub to his baby sister, Darius once sighed "Back the **** up." Or, when startled by a sudden movement, he'd say, "What the ****?" They stated these phrases the same way other little children would say, "Move, please" or "Whoa!"

Their vocabulary made public outings risky trips. First, their words for body parts caused jaw-dropping responses from strangers (and me!), so when they saw the undergarments section of Target, they erupted with R-rated material and giggles. I could only chuckle along—yet another proof that teenagers had raised these little children thus far. Their cursing drove Jack and Ariel nuts because I expected Jack and Ariel, as middle schoolers, to use appropriate language, but the little ones had no punishment for their filthy vernacular.

As TJ mentioned earlier, we normally gave children a "grace period" when they came in the home, and we gradually enforced standards as they grew accustomed to us. However, we did not create a rigid protocol for bringing new children into our family. I suppose that is the answer: treat every child and situation uniquely. With these two, we decided to let it slide because we had other foundations to focus on.

The first month we cared for Darius and Jasmine, we only disciplined for flagrant violations of social norms. That alone was a full-time job. I remember squatting beside Darius in time-out at least a dozen times one day for hitting other kids or stealing their toys at a play date. Another week, almost every time we would go toward the van, Darius bolted down the sidewalk in the opposite direction, laughing. A stuffed animal backpack with a tail for a leash worked miracles.

Then, Darius's Sunday school teacher pulled me aside once to say I could no longer bring him unless I would stay in class with him. Another pulled TJ aside to share about Darius's language in class.

We intentionally let certain bad behavior slide so we could focus on others. You eat an elephant one bite at a time, right?

A few months in, cursing faded from their vocabulary. One night, well past bedtime, I walked up to Darius's door, about to don my firm mommy voice to say, "Shhh! Quit talking and go to bed! You'll wake the baby!" but I heard him singing, "Kumbaya my Lord…Kumbaya." I cherished the sounds and just sat against the door to listen instead. And like many little ones, they eventually would tattle on Woody in Toy Story or TJ when they said stupid, declaring, "Awwwwwwww…Woody said a bad wwwwoooorrrrrd."

Soon, Darius helped younger children in his Sunday school class and reached out his hand to hold hands as we crossed the street together. The giggles in the bra section continued, of course.

When Jasmine came, besides the cursing, she danced provocatively—spread legs, hands down on the coffee table, shaking-her-booty kind of moves. She was four. Should she have been scolded? No, she was testing the water to see if this was okay here. I shook my head and showed her some appropriate dance moves to do instead. In my home, she had plenty of opportunities to dance, and I saw her watching and modeling my own sweet moves or mimicking Angelina the mouse ballerina.

TJ

Sleep terrors are awful. Perhaps one of the more sobering aspects of parenting hurt children involves tending to their unconscious expressions of fear and anxiety while sleeping. This is commonly referred to as "night terrors." A few children we cared for released blood-curdling screams in their sleep and refused comfort. Jasmine's terrors seemed like the worst, both in frequency and intensity.

I felt sorry and sympathetic for Jasmine whenever she experienced these dreams, but I also felt anger. She was the oldest sibling of probably the most traumatized group of children we ever welcomed into our home. I felt angry at the mother who neglected and abused her. The mother's actions caused Jasmine to experience things no one should ever have to face, certainly not a child. And honestly, some nights I felt tired and frustrated at Jasmine's inability to calm herself down or receive comfort.

The child welfare system also failed Jasmine. The state allowed them to remain in a filthy, one-room house with no running water for over a year as marks on their bodies accumulated, all under the premise of "family preservation." Keeping children in abusive situations preserves no one.

Jasmine's reactions were different from simply having a "bad dream." Most children recognize bad dreams as figments of their imaginations within a few minutes. I believe Jasmine recalled traumatic events she actually experienced, which triggered other fearful thoughts. She woke up, but the memory of these events did not disappear. Her body had scars as physical proof of her past abuse. Her terrors were evidence of unseen emotional scars.

We tried different techniques to calm Jasmine down when her night terrors struck. At first, we attributed it to her presence in a new place with unfamiliar people. Quickly, we realized she was suffering through something much worse than mere discomfort. Jasmine frequently woke up screaming and sobbing, refusing comfort.

Jenn and I both attempted to reassure her of our presence and concern while sitting on the side of her bed, but it didn't help. She literally cried and moaned for an hour or more some nights. Maybe she was fighting to stay awake to avoid the experience of another terror. Jasmine's limited vocabulary, along with her inability to articulate what she felt, undoubtedly led to more isolation. She could not communicate what was wrong, and we did not understand the depth of her fear.

Eventually, as we began to understand Jasmine's personality and her background better, we changed our response to her night terrors. Jenn and I took turns going to her room, holding her like an infant in our arms, and singing softly to her. Even though she was in kindergarten, Jasmine enjoyed being held, treated, and spoken to like a baby. She demonstrated clear signs that she had not had many of her infant needs met, and cradling her like a baby helped soothe her fear and anxiety.

Gradually, these sessions dwindled from an hour or more, to half an hour, to fifteen minutes, to just a couple minutes. Thankfully, through God's redemptive work in her life, Jasmine also experienced fewer night terrors, and as her English improved, she could even tell us what she wanted or understand what we were asking her. By the time she left our home, night terrors rarely occurred. I am thankful God used a combination of love, therapy, and time in a safe environment to free Jasmine of these traumatic episodes.

Jenn

With time, some foster children became so well-adjusted that someone wouldn't know their hurt histories. I often made the dangerous mistake of comparing the lives and progress of foster children to typical children.

I like to read, so I naturally sought out plenty of parenting books. I also observed my mom friends and what they did with their kids. I longed for afternoons of music lessons instead of therapy, or working on "Finish your dinner" rather than finding food stuffed throughout their room. I trained my thoughts to constantly recenter on the truth that these children often needed healing, not discipline.

One week, I found myself frustrated with Jasmine's and Darius's inability to go through a morning routine without paralyzing into tears, making them late for school. I rationalized, "They've been with us a year" as justification for my expectations of perfect behavior. Infant-like breakdowns for no apparent reason, crocodile tears appearing at every transition of activity, straight defiance in school-aged children, and on-the-floor-banging-around tantrums became the norm again. I started losing my patience for it, thinking, Ugh, we have been here before. We've already done this!

Many of their days consisted of the same activities as a typical child of their ages, so in the day-to-day grind, I somehow forgot their background, how their situation felt uncertain and scary. It had to be exhausting. I found the Holy Spirit reminding me, "Throw the books away and stop comparing your kids or your parenting. Just follow My lead."

I identified that their behavior frustrated me because it was a regression of a year's worth of behavior improvement. I realized, They resumed birth parent visits—duh. After months without seeing any birth parent, for the last three weeks, I drove them an afternoon each week to spend with their birth mom and dad. Of course that would upset children at a deep level.

The Holy Spirit led me to embrace this junk with "time-ins" of holding tightly in hugs multiple times a day, fun in response to fits, and letting a lot of behavior slide, as much as the just judge inside me said, "No, no, NO!"

The clear regression in Jasmine and Darius also helped me empathize with Jack and Ariel. Jack and I spent extra time together playing games every day and talking in the evening long past bedtime, even though he was suspended from school, and I felt the conventional parenting pressure to think, "He should be grounded."

One evening after dinner, Jasmine broke down in sobs of defeat while sweeping for a couple minutes, a chore the children rotated doing while their siblings bathed. Music was on and I washed dishes beside her, but she just didn't want to sweep. I tried cheering her on to persevere, "Jasmine's mama's helper tonight: You're just like mommy cleaning up, and, wow, you're almost done already!" but that only brought her to the cusp of crying out. I took a deep breath to keep from sighing, scooped her up like a toddler, sat on a kitchen chair and hugged her tight.

She silenced, the music played, and I took deep breaths of surrender as I sort of spaced out, tired, too. I tuned into the song lyric, just as the lyrics started repeating softly in J.J. Heller's soothing voice, "Have mercy on me; I'm not what I used to be."[20] Four minutes later, of breathing together and hearts beating, I kissed Jasmine, and said, "Let's finish and then read a book together." She almost smiled, hopped up, and swept super-fast, and then off we went happy campers.

Kids with relatively carefree lives have breakdowns. How much more so for kids in constant tension? Jasmine needed space to express her deep grief, confusion, and exhaustion. Who knows what thoughts stuck in her mind? Even with all the love and stability we provided, her future was cloudy, and the circumstances felt like a tornado she had no control over.

TJ

God provided a neat event for me to cherish with Jasmine. My unit hosted a daddy-daughter ball where my commander and his wife dressed as a king and queen. There was a red carpet, formal introductions, and fancy food. Jasmine wore a beautiful white princess dress, complete with arm-length gloves and a tiara. I wore my most formal military uniform, Jenn took photos, and as we left the house, Jasmine grinned from ear to ear.

She didn't say a single word the entire fifteen-minute drive to the ball. Whenever I would ask her a question, silence followed. She was so nervous, she would see me looking at her, grin, and then turn away and stare out the window of my truck. Her hands anxiously moved from her lap, to her arms, to her face, and back again. Once we arrived and walked into the hotel, she started to relax. Then we turned the corner, and she saw a woman dressed as a princess with the king and queen standing a few yards behind.

Jasmine was overwhelmed with wonder, but her face broke into an enormous smile. The princess asked our names and led us to the red carpet, where soldiers with sabers in their dress uniforms lined either side. She tightened her grip on my hand as we waited for the formal announcement of our arrival to the ball, "Your Majesty, Sir TJ and Princess Jasmine"

The soldiers raised their sabers creating an archway for us to walk through, with the king and queen waiting to welcome us on the other side. Jasmine was in awe of her surroundings and could not bring herself to speak more than just a simple "yes" when the queen asked if she was enjoying herself.

We made our way to a private table, and I watched as she devoured her meal in a very non-princess-like manner, but that was Jasmine—she really enjoyed her food. After dinner, we danced to a few songs, took a trolley ride through downtown, and posed for pictures before departing. She was much more talkative on the way home, but as we turned into our neighborhood, she let out a yawn. I will never forget the wonderful evening, and I hope it's one which crowds out other not-so-pleasant evenings of her past.

Jenn

One warm spring weekend, I ventured to the beach with Jasmine, Darius, and Tamika while TJ was off saving the world. The first time we went to the beach shortly after Jasmine and Darius came, they clung and clawed to TJ and me like a cat avoiding a bath. We did not force them into the water; in fact, we were over one hundred yards away from the waves. Just the sight of the ocean evoked such fear. Plenty of kids played around happily, but for the first half dozen trips to the beach, Jasmine and Darius wore fear, caution, and skepticism on their faces.

This time, something broke free in Jasmine. At least three months had passed, maybe five, since our final beach trip before winter. In those months, God worked in that child. To my surprise, there at low tide, Jasmine sprinted toward the water, prancing on bubbles, and spinning in circles like a ballerina (insert my deep sigh of pride). She stomped puddles and shouted in delight as she chased birds. All by herself. Brave.

God knew I needed this evident portrayal of her life change. I love Jesus. I love His healing power in her little life, and how it shows itself in sweet moments.

In the midst of the grind of school and conversations with all sorts of professionals about all the areas in which Jasmine was behind and struggling, she felt free. No more booty dancing and fear. What a display of magnificence, to see little Jasmine spinning freely before God's big creation. Every time I recall this memory, my eyes swell with sweet tears. I miss her.

So even though children face complicated situations and foster parents will encounter setbacks, the potential for positive impact in children, and the gratification when it's reached, far outweighs the frustrations. The excerpt below is from a school teacher's court testimony and came at a particular time when I felt out of control of most variables in Jasmine's life:

The differences I have seen in the children since placement are truly remarkable. When I first met Jasmine she would not talk to or make eye contact with me, other workers, or even other children. It was very difficult to get her to engage in any way, and when she did, it was with one-word responses. Much of the time she would sit with two fingers in her mouth, her knees pulled to her chest, sometimes making crying noises somewhat like that of a small puppy. Somber and withdrawn are two words I would use to describe Jasmine at that time...

The transformation I have seen in Jasmine since they have been with the Menns has been dramatic. Jasmine is a true little girl. She loves to dress up and is always ready to model her dress or shoes. She loves other children and plays well with them. Although a little shy, she makes eye contact and readily engages in conversation and participates in activities. Jasmine laughs easily now, something it took months to see...I know it probably sounds like the changes are exaggerated, but they are not.

I feel the changes can be directly attributed to the unconditional love and stability Jenn and TJ have given them. I barely knew Jenn and TJ before [this case], but have developed a relationship and great respect for them during this time...There is no doubt that she is thriving.

Even when I felt out of control and helpless, Jasmine's life changed. God's love and provision during a time of chaos in her life created a refuge for growth to occur.

Takeaways

The amount of brokenness passed down through generations of foster children is staggering. Without an intentional effort to redirect their path, children in the foster care system are almost doomed. In some states, up to fifty percent of the homeless population and eighty percent of incarcerated individuals spent time in foster care as children.[21] Another study shows about one in four former foster children need public assistance as adults during at least some point of their adulthood.[22]

Foster parents can intercede early to help shape lives. What better time to address the problems of poverty, homelessness, crime, and abuse than before they're ingrained in the minds and lives of little ones? People often do what others model for them, and although children may have come into our care with the "baggage" of exposure to harmful environments, they can change. Even temporary living in a healthy environment can result in a lifetime of change.

As you may have noticed, this chapter mentioned discipline. Many of our friends who are parents comment, "I don't know how you do it without being able to spank." Without going off on too much of a tangent, we'd like to share with you some thoughts.

First, foster parenting requires trying out all sorts of love and discipline. If a parent cannot overcome the belief that spanking is the only form of effective discipline, then foster parenting will feel like trying to slam a star-shaped peg into a circular hole. It won't work, and it may hurt. Foster children represent exceptions to many parenting generalities.

Most Christians desire to raise children who respect authority, which is important. While Proverbs speaks of the value of "the rod" for teaching authority, it's not the only tool for training. When adults become foster parents, they too are under the authority of both the government and Jesus. The government says no physical discipline, period. Foster parents cannot hypocritically spank foster children and thus claim to teach their children obedience while disregarding the government's instructions to refrain from the physical discipline of foster children.

More importantly, Jesus says He can help. The God who is able to deliver Daniel from a lion's den, Peter from prison, and part the

Red Sea[23] can totally provide us with insight and means to accomplish what He has asked of us in parenting. Countless times we asked the Holy Spirit, "Okay, what are we supposed to do?" or we simply felt His leading to respond in circumstances. We're not exaggerating. Countless times.

Parents are also generally concerned about doing the right thing and ensuring their kids are moral. However, parents can become a bit caught up in enforcing righteousness in their children. "Be perfect and obey" is a tall order. These babes need grace and love. They need to know, "Jesus loves them, and, therefore, we love them, too." Parents coddle infants in this way for months. Foster children may need that sort of coddling in the beginning. This may mean "allowing for" certain despicable behavior in these children for a season. The state of a child's heart is more important than his behavior.

Some parents genuinely ask us, "Well, then, what do you do?!" as if no other methods of behavior modification exist. Let us assure you, lots of forms of effective discipline exist such as time-outs, taking away toys, positive reinforcement, or assigning extra chores. They might not seem as convenient if spanking is a parent's all-in-one tool for discipline. Foster parent training classes discuss options at length, and even more importantly, God will not leave His followers empty-handed. He cares about both His children's behavior and their hearts.[24]

Oftentimes, we felt more constrained by random policies than disciplinary restrictions. Oh, blessed policies. They told us where to keep dish soap, the number of smoke detectors we had to have, what types of responses we should give to homosexuals, and anything else under the sun. If we overlooked a detail and a social worker or birth parent observed parenting they disagreed with, a social worker could simply write a memo and force us to comply by threatening to take the children away. An amber teething necklace or delaying vaccines is just as taboo as spanking.

To be honest, foster parenting can feel like walking through life with your hands tied behind your back in lots of areas. The state, birth parents, and foster parents all have opinions on how to best raise the child, and all think their opinion is the most important one to listen to. Humility comes in handy.

Of course it's hard. When we felt like quitting, we recalled that foster parenting represented a tremendous opportunity to build up young lives and serve the community's most precious resource: the children. Experiencing life with the kids far outweighed the strain. Fostering can be a challenge, but almost anything worth pursuing is difficult.

Chapter 9

When We Don't Look Alike

"The bloodline of Jesus is thicker, deeper, stronger than the bloodline of race, ethnicity, and family."
—John Piper[25]

Jenn

I'm not even going to try to thoroughly address the scope of blending races in a family. Bookstores have racks on the subject. But I will say becoming a transracial family stirred the pot around me in a new way. About half of our foster children shared our race and half represented other races. We never chose placements based on color and often had no idea of the children's race until after we welcomed them into our home.

As a mom, I met individual needs and nurtured them. Every child is unique, so each child's diet, skin, or health care may have different needs. Yet all kids need love and acceptance of the way God chose to make us. Racial identity is valuable, but the daily nurturing of the child through loving commitment can happen regardless of race. Interracial and transracial families continue to demonstrate the beauty of diversity in family.

When we had a mixed family composition, public responses ranged from humorous comments, like children asserting, "Your man must be so black!" to leading questions about my pregnancies or assuming I ran a day care. Comments rarely offended the children or TJ and me. People mostly spoke out of curiosity, with a pinch of unsolicited advice on hair braiding.

Sometimes, I felt women of similar race as the children watching me like a hawk. Other times, strangers gave commands to my children with me present as if simply sharing the same race placed them in a relationship greater than mine. Is this cultural? Is this intentional? If I looked like I could've given birth to them, would I face the same situation? I struggled to respond to implicit biases or microaggressions. These behaviors are frustrating because they are hard to explain to others, yet wreak havoc.

TJ

Bringing any foster child into our family created challenges. Welcoming a child of a different race probably presented a few more. I mention these additional difficulties in an effort to raise awareness, not to discourage transracial foster families. This sensitive subject has very divergent opinions, and only you can determine the correct situation for your family.

Caring for children of a different race changed our life, but not all the changes were positive. Racial tensions keep causing harm to all races and all ages. Some people reading this book will think it's ridiculous I even wrote the previous sentence because, for them, racial tensions have been a constant part of their life. There are other folks who are on the other extreme and have no experience with racial tension at all in their daily lives. I know this is true because I used to experience very little racial diversity. Growing up in the rural Midwest does not exactly represent the "melting pot" America is known for.

We walked into the transracial situation blindly. As such, we acted insensitively to racial expectations yet defended our own cultural parenting choices. It felt uncomfortable and jarring. The various parties communicated terribly. I know we felt as if we walked on eggshells, constantly concerned something we said would be twisted and used against us. These circumstances caused a lot of pain and discomfort, but they will not prevent us from caring for any children in the future. We are hopeful the foster care system—and the country—will continue to improve in the area of race relations.

I think I was pretty naïve about the state of race relations in America. Even though African Americans comprised a majority of my first platoon, I forgot society doesn't always function with the same team mentality as an army unit. The reactions of case managers and the public at large surprised me when we cared for a child of a different race. It took a while before I adjusted to the stares and hushed whispering that took place whenever we took our mixed-race family out in public. I do believe, however, these types of reactions are diminishing as transracial families become more common.

To those who read this book and consider fostering, I would strongly suggest an open and honest conversation with your spouse about race. When the social worker calls with an emergency placement of a child, you should know your feelings on this issue. It is perfectly fine to inquire about the race of the child before you make a decision, although the case manager may not know. You should not feel pressure to parent a different race child, nor do you need to limit your home to children of your own race. You know better than anyone else the attitudes, situations, and people this child will encounter when living with you. Discussing the topic with your family will help solidify your thinking on the matter. It will also help you articulate your reasoning if your motives are questioned.

---------- *Takeaways* ----------

In an area like transracial placement where emotions run high and opinions frequently differ, open and honest communication is essential. Even when we disagreed with case managers' decisions, knowing the logic behind the decision or hearing the facts helps interactions.

Chaos ensues when people hide motives. Without a doubt, racially-driven social workers wreaked the most havoc on our lives and the lives of the children in our care. Federal law states that social workers cannot rule out an adoptive or foster family placement because of race. It still happens, but now through loopholes, false accusations, or microaggression. For example, a nationwide group called the National Association of Black Social Workers, with many active local chapters, is working against transracial placements regarding black children in non-black homes. Their reasoning is below.

The National Association of Black Social Workers has taken a vehement stand against the placement of Black children in white homes for any reason. We affirm the inviolable position of Black children in Black families where they belong physically, psychologically, and culturally in order that they receive the total sense of themselves and develop a sound projection of their futures…Black children in white homes are cut off from the healthy development of themselves as Black people, which development is the normal expectation and only true humanistic goal.26

This quote is from their current position statement on transracial adoption, which is unchanged since 1972 (at the time of our writing in 2016). Ideology acts as an internal force, greater than the law, to perpetuate conflict. Active members of this group served in our county, came into our home, and judged our parenting harshly to the point where witnesses—a counselor, a lawyer, and a mother in a waiting room—all shared their concern with how the worker treated us disrespectfully.

Based on the social worker's idea of the "best interests of the child," they can (and did) move children away from settled placements based on general well-being into "best" placements defined as such only because they represent same race placements. Even recent legislation such as the Adoption Safe Families Act includes a clause used to continue the practice of race-based placement in some areas of America, though technically race-based discrimination in foster care placement is illegal.

State and federal laws explain general rules of operation for child welfare such as timelines and how children are treated in care, but they leave a whole lot of room for interpretation. Then, the Department of Child Services in different states writes policies as to how they interpret the law. These policies leave freedom for staff of the department to decide what's in the best interest of a child. This is sensible and allows professionals to use common sense on a case by case basis.

However, one unfortunate result of this governance is the opportunity for a strongly-biased social worker to make poor decisions without accountability. Case managers can even circumvent a court-appointed judge who says they are out of their right minds.

We have a vivid memory of a smug case manager walking out of a courtroom muttering, "Ugh, that judge, who does she think she is? Telling us what to do!"

We don't mean to criticize case managers. We would be lost without them. Thousands upon thousands of committed professionals in the social and legal fields work hard to identify and ensure children's best interests. They answer calls and run out to tend to emergencies at all hours of the night. They step into social tornadoes and sketchy places every day. We love you.

Even though this chapter seems discouraging, a lot of progress has transpired in the last decade or two. While race may still enter into consideration when talking about the ideal family for a child, at least foster parents can now adopt. For most of the history of the foster care system, foster parents were prohibited from adopting their foster children. Now, they often have the first chance to adopt the children after family members. Secondly, discrimination against transracial placements is illegal, although caveats for the child's "best interest" still remain. Lastly, Congress enacted a firm time frame on how long children should have to wait for their birth parents to show progress before a judge can terminate the birth parent's rights. The limit is now fifteen months, though often judges grant more time.[27] All of these measures help move children from foster care into permanent homes.

Chapter 10
Always Waiting

"A man's wisdom gives him patience; it is to his glory to overlook an offense."

— Proverbs 19:11

Jenn

Think about a time in your life when you waited for important news. Maybe you sat in a hospital tapping your foot anxiously waiting for the doctor to share news, or watched a big game calling out "Come on, come on!" during the final minutes. Waiting can feel miserable. When we wait to hear information, especially where we have little control, anxiety builds up, showing itself in stomach flutters, chest tightening, nail biting, or lip chewing.

Foster parenting is a constant waiting game. We wait for calls to welcome children. We wait for their arrival. We wait for information and assessments on them. We wait for visits to come around. We wait for court dates. We wait for the day they can return home. We care for the kids while they wait to see if their parents will rehabilitate or not. We feel the tension and so do the kids.

I have a hard time telling a story about waiting because when a story reads, it happens so quickly that it's an injustice to the exhaustion of day in and day out waiting for week after week. Time lapses are strange. Spend a moment and think of a personal example to help wrap your mind around eighteen months. What were you doing a year and a half ago? Pull out a picture of a child you love from eighteen months ago. Count the days.

About a year after having Jasmine, Darius, and Tamika in our home, their case manager asked us if we would consider adopting them if the courts terminated the parents' rights. We agreed. In another six months, the new case manager notified us he had started the paper work for terminating the birth parents' rights with the court. And so we waited.

The process is pretty lengthy. First, the case manager needed to pull together evidence to show that the state gave the parents at least a year to try and yet they're still unfit to parent. Then, he must submit the large packet for review and wait for several supervisors within the bureaucracy to read the stack. Then, of course, a week of training, a week of vacation, and a week of catching up would occur before reviewing up the packet.

At that point, the case manager would receive the packet back with revisions. He would resubmit the packet and finally submit it to the court. We would all wait for the court to set a date, at least six weeks away, to give the sheriff's office time to serve the parents the hearing papers.

While we waited, I wrote in my journal:

I eagerly wait for the complete fulfillment of my adoption as God's child—the doubt, discouragement, disunity, disease all to pass away. I long to enter into a full and complete relationship with God where the strongholds of the flesh wipe away and eternal life comes into full bloom.

I also eagerly wait for the adoption of my foster children. I doubt it will happen. I feel discouraged by the circumstances and obstacles. Disunity between all involved parties runs rampant: birth parents, foster parents, professional team, the state's child welfare department. These children carry generational issues I sense can heal only when physical adoption takes place and we can bring them into our family covenant. This limbo parenting feels tense. Likewise, our time in the world is tense and subject to the spiritual powers under the god of this age.

I comprehend eagerness. The anticipation draws us near to trusting God's sovereignty... "Who hopes for what he already has?" implies intense hope that my perception of the best outcome will roll out well. It's the suspense in a good movie that has your stomach churning and telling yourself, "Surely the good guy can't die."

What's the difference between eagerness and impatience? Eagerness flows from hopeful anticipation where impatience flows from aggravated discontentment. One trusts the Lord where the latter is bothered by the Lord's timing and purposes.

When I foster, I feel this. I understand it in a way I couldn't possibly before. It's palpable. Fostering is sanctifying me. It's like seeing this world's limbo, temporary state from God the Father's point of view.

I don't know what will happen, but I hope whatever may come, God's grace will be there. His grace will bring the kids and us love, joy, peace, patience, kindness, gentleness, faithfulness, and self-control. He will give me the power to do anything in His will through His Holy Spirit living in me. That's amazing, and I don't ever want to step out from that hope.

TJ

The bureaucratic hurdles, arbitrary supervisor decisions, and case manager mistakes with Jasmine, Darius, and Tamika's case seemed countless. The Bible extols patience in many books, yet I struggle to obtain it when a matter is close to my heart. I felt out of control and forced to accept decisions with enormous consequence upon the futures of the children in our home without any input. Anger seemed more appealing and even more appropriate than patience. How could I trust the state's process to produce the best result for the children when they changed to a fifth case manager in less than a year?

Patience does not necessarily mean silence, however. As caretakers, we engaged intimately in the day-to-day lives of the children. Although we only saw one angle of the case, we vocally advocated for the needs and desires of the children in our custody. Some people welcomed this participation while others seemed to stop up their ears.

We also practiced patience with the rate of birth parents' progress because it often disappointed us. Since family restoration is the first priority of foster care, the progress of parents stays in the spotlight. Patience and prayer helped me empathize with the parents' difficulties as well as keep the overall goal of reunification in the forefront of my mind.

Finally, patience helped us operate in a system where the average time children remain in foster care is twenty-one months.[28] National law sets a standard for children to exit foster care within fifteen months because leaders recognize prolonged waiting causes damage. However, inefficiencies, overloaded case managers, and lack of resources all combine to create a painfully slow process. I wish I could offer a simple solution for handling the exasperation of delays, mistakes, or incompetence that hurt the children.

Part of my distress came from a righteous anger; I wanted the kids placed in a loving, safe, permanent home as soon as possible. However, I probably felt more frustration than I like to admit over unmet expectations, which resulted in agonizing disappointment. When a distant character made decisions we disagreed with, submitting to the state's authority felt unnatural. I reacted in frustration instead of taking my arguments to God in prayer.

Jenn

Hope helped us persevere. It's a supernatural gift to get us through hard times. Hope is substantial and crucial, yet also abstract and hard to identify when we're feeling it.

After having Jasmine, Darius, and Tamika with us for so long, people often asked, "Are you going to adopt them?" I started wondering, "Am I? I hope so." And that seemed like an appropriate answer: "I hope so." Could I say I didn't hope so? That didn't sound appropriate. When hope for the birth parents at this point seemed in vain, what hope did we have for the kids?

Jasmine wanted to understand her future and feel safe, so she asked if she would live with us forever. She also asked, "Am I your daughter?" with inquisitive eyes. How could I give assurance of love, be honest, but not breed insecurity?

We waited for all sorts of answers, and not just to the long term permanency question. Will their birth mom show up for the weekly visit? Will the parents grant permission for holiday travel? Will their birth mom complete rehab? I hoped so.

People who did life with us wanted answers, too. And though I felt in shaky limbo with the situation, "I don't know" is not always an acceptable answer. Repeating "I don't know" seems to require a follow-up explanation of why I don't know. It creates tension in conversation with others, and saying "I don't know" again and again builds feelings of insecurity.

I wanted to provide assurance. I had to learn to take to heart and communicate to others "Only God knows" and nothing more. I meant this sincerely, not flippantly. All we can hope for is God's grace to be revealed. Whatever we faced, whether little disappointments or tearing up a family, we hoped God gave the children and all involved grace. In 1 Peter 1:13, Peter writes, "Set your hope fully on the grace of Jesus Christ to be revealed." To keep all my hope in Christ when my desires tug in other directions required faith, trust, and disciplined obedience.

And, frankly, I failed. A big change occurred when I started choosing new names for them in my mind. Or when friends adopted their placements from foster care, and it seemed like we had traveled a very similar path. Or when a child's therapist gave me suggestions about decor for an adoption party. None of these people had ill intentions, but they all reinforced the pull to place my hope somewhere other than on the grace of Jesus Christ.

TJ

With the strain of waiting constantly hanging over the family, we tried to keep life full of activity and fun. I'm a farm kid, so we don't do indoor pets. When Jenn asked for a dog. I said, "We already have chickens in the backyard."

She countered, "An indoor dog would help bring healing to the kids in ways we can't. So much research backs it up. Come on. Don't write it off just because you don't want an animal inside the house." Despite my opposition, I agreed to pray about the decision.

I usually run several mornings a week, and one day, shortly after our discussion, I had the idea to stop by our neighbor's horse farm about a mile away. I had never met the owners, but found the setting of the farm intriguing. Their farm is located inside the city limits but tucked away on a street I only found through running. Woods surrounded most of the pasture, and a small pond sat in the middle of the property next to the barn.

Thankfully, as I ran by the fence line, I spotted a woman performing some morning chores, so I went over and introduced myself. During the course of the conversation, I asked about exchanging my labor on the farm for some time around the horses, chickens, and dog with the kids.

I explained that I had not spent a lot of time with horses; my family raised mostly hogs, cattle, or chickens, but I knew stalls needed cleaning fairly often and, "I can scoop poop with the best of them." She said, "Of course!" and provided the times she would be at the farm.

The first time we visited the farm, the kids had a blast. They enjoyed feeding the horses, helping to scoop sawdust into the stalls, and riding around the pasture on a John Deere Gator. At first, the dog, named Sconset, terrified them. Maybe they had a bad experience with dogs, or maybe Sconset's large size scared them. Regardless of the reason, Sconset's gentle nature and continual appetite for fetch soon won over the kids. I'm not sure who wore the other out first, the dog from chasing sticks or the kids from throwing them.

The children also took part in meaningful chores around the farm which helped them assume a small amount of responsibility. Sharing the burden of caring for these animals, however small the contribution, brought a sense of belonging and pride in completing a task. Whenever a guest came along, they sprinted ahead of the group to the barn and led a tour, talking the person's ear off (usually another farmer) about the different animals.

The consistency of a farm and exposure to the gentle spirit of the horses and the dog worked therapeutic wonders in the lives of the children. The routine of the farm provided joy and growth for the kids while we lived in a constant state of uncertainty.

Takeaways

We found waiting to be one of the more difficult aspects of foster care, and while distractions and routine helped, prayer is the strongest antidote. We can express our feelings of helplessness or frustration to God in prayer. God brings about miraculous results through the power of prayer. We often prayed for wisdom, discernment, resolution, and restoration.

First, we asked God to grant wisdom. We requested His wisdom for the case managers and all the officials who handled the case. We asked for parents to receive His wisdom. We also asked Him for wisdom in parenting and caring for the children in our home.

Secondly, we asked God for discernment. As mentioned earlier, we recognized our view of the case was limited to the perspective of the children in our home. We prayed for God to grant us discernment in knowing His will for the children and their future. Again, we did not limit this prayer to ourselves but included everyone involved in the case. Judges, lawyers, and case managers make decisions every day that literally change lives. Discernment helps when deliberating any course of action, certainly when children's futures are at stake.

We asked the Lord for the resolution of our cases. We tried to remain open to whatever outcome God led us to rather than fixing our mind on what we thought best. This prayer certainly included the children in our care, who often needed to confront feelings of anger, betrayal, sadness, or many other emotions related to their situation.

Finally, we requested restoration. We prayed for restoration of the family as well as for the relationships damaged in the difficult and painful process. In cases where complete family restoration was impossible, we asked God to give the individuals involved the strength and courage to forgive. Many times, we prayed for the restoration of a right relationship between the parents and God.

Prayer builds patience, and foster parents are given plenty of opportunities to exercise this cyclical growth. We attempted to practice patience amidst frustrating circumstances, and we hope the world saw a difference in our lives.

Chapter 11

Broken Promises

"We think sometimes that poverty is only being hungry, naked, and homeless. The poverty of being unwanted, unloved, and uncared for is the greatest poverty. We must start in our own homes to remedy this kind of poverty."
—Mother Teresa[29]

Jenn

Jack spoke of the happiest time of his childhood as "When we lived in a purple house...like a real house in town...and went to school every day, and we could walk to the library." But soon the cupboards emptied. The water turned off. Jack asked the neighbor if they could use his hose to drink. One time, he and Ariel were home alone and so thirsty they drank maple-flavored syrup. Before long, they ended up at a campsite with their parents' friends. The school bus route didn't come that far, so the kids did not attend school. The purple house became a faraway dream.

A child's entry into foster care usually brings numerous heartbreaks. Besides the obvious trauma of leaving their parents, the children lose their friends, neighbors, and almost everything familiar to them. In addition, the children visit their birth parents regularly, have their hopes raised for returning home, and then, all too often, these hopes are crushed when a court proceeding is delayed or a parent fails a drug test. This cycle of anticipation followed by disappointment continues for months or even years. It is often repeated with more mundane promises like future phone calls or gifts. Eventually, the children's outcome is determined for them. Some children have anxiety and dread about returning home, fearing additional trauma or abuse. While waiting, many children move between shelters or foster homes and feel like a commodity. It's an emotional typhoon.

Shortly after Jack and Ariel moved in with us, their dad got out of jail, moved to town, swept them off their feet, and brought them into a cute, stable home. Oh, no, wait, he only promised those things. Instead, he got out of jail, shot up heroin, and got arrested. The case manager informed me of the news and then told me to "have the kids' therapist tell them" this devastating news.

Well, we had just changed the kids' therapist after she overloaded them on psychotropic medications at their previous placement, so that wasn't an option. TJ was across the world at war and out of reach.

I prayed about how to share the news, knowing it could devastate them. Because of their dad's decision, the kids would stay in foster care a minimum of six more months. Their expectations were already sky-high because of the hope their father's empty promises had created. Their time in foster care consisted of a shelter first and then two foster homes over the last fourteen months.

Do you remember being in fourth grade looking into the future at middle schoolers? It seemed forever away. Think about the many changes in a child over just a few months. I pondered this in my heart and didn't set a date to tell them, but waited for an opportune time in the coming days.

God helped in several ways, of course.

First, I listened to an audio book called *The Glass Castle*,[30] which is the memoir of a young girl in a dysfunctional family suffering from homelessness, alcoholism, and a dad who broke a lot of promises. Ariel caught me listening to a couple minutes of it one day when I picked her up from school. I started to turn it off because of some adult content, but Ariel exclaimed, "No way!" Here she found a girl she related to, and she could also objectively observe how the character behaved.

So, over the course of the month, we listened to the story together. I drove over a half hour each way to Ariel's school so she could remain in the school she attended when she had moved into our home. We had plenty of time each afternoon to listen and discuss the girls' somewhat similar journey.

Secondly, I saw a preview for the movie *Like Dandelion Dust*. It popped up on RedBox when the three of us went to pick out a DVD for movie night. I told the kids about the movie's premise, and they wanted to rent it. I felt a bit cautious knowing the movie contained a lot of adoption-related storylines. They begged with pouting lips. I gave in.

The plot of the movie centers on a birth father whose son was placed for adoption as an infant while he was in prison, unbeknownst to him. When the father gets out of prison five years later, he ends up discovering the news about the boy and starts fighting for custody of him. All the while, his son has grown up with a wholesome, affluent couple who adopted him and loved him very much. The movie plays out the drama of all the questions: Who has parental rights to this son? What's best for the boy? Does that matter?

Watching the movie brought up great conversations about what defines a parent as well as what's right and wrong in parenting. In the movie, the dad breaks a lot of promises when he is addicted to drugs, but you also see the love he has for his son. During the movie, the kids and I discussed some tough decisions the movie characters faced and what they would have done.

At the conclusion of the movie, I knew the Lord set me up to share the hard news about their dad. The moment I broke the news, Jack crumpled into a fetal position and sobbed. Sobbed. The only words heard from him through the groans were, "But he promised." That moment is branded in my mind.

Ariel went wide-eyed and somber looking but didn't understand. She quietly asked, "What's heroin?"

Jack shouted at her, "HOW STUPID CAN YOU BE?!"

By then, I'd already crawled over to Jack to comfort him. I tried to encourage him, "Jack, what a good big brother you've been. You protected her so well from so much of the junk going on around you that she doesn't even know what heroin is! Wow."

Then I explained more of the situation in Ariel's terms so that she could understand, and she too cried, saying, "He promised me not to smoke again!" Jack vented about his anger at his dad. He determined to confront his dad about it. Even in the coming days, he wanted to let his dad know how much it disappointed him. He told his case manager as well, but week after week at his visitation, he said, "It was never the right time. I didn't want to ruin the fun."

Their parents habitually broke promises. After a visit, Ariel would announce the newest promises with pride. "My parents said when we get back together next month…" or "By my birthday…" we'll do this or that. They marked calendars, told friends, and clung to their parents' words. The kids' behavior in our house started going downhill the longer they lingered in care, when the dates of many of these promises came and went and were scribbled out on the calendar.

New promises came as frequently as the old ones expired. Ariel prayed diligently to be with her parents by an upcoming "final" court date. The possibility of reuniting looked pretty bleak, but judges often give more leeway for parents in cases with older children. Naturally, older kids have more years of memories, while also facing a smaller chance of adoption.

The case worker asked us if we would consider adopting the children, unbeknownst to the children or parents. He needed a backup plan in case the birth parents failed. When TJ returned from a deployment, the two of us scheduled a night away at a beach house and finally had time to discuss the decision. Through much prayer, TJ and I determined we would love to adopt them if necessary, but we remained committed to helping the family come back together.

TJ

Coming to this determination took God's direction. How could we balance a commitment to adopt while maintaining a commitment to parental reunification? It sounds easier conceptually than it is emotionally.

King David is a famous character in the Bible who ruled over the nation of Israel. He is known as a man who followed God's heart. When Jenn and I considered adopting Jack and Ariel, we recalled a biblical passage about David's life and thought the Holy Spirit used it to help guide our decision.

Samuel, an Old Testament prophet, anointed David the next king of Israel when David was pretty young, yet David still diligently honored the current king, Saul.[31] David had several opportunities to take the kingdom by force while Saul acted defensively and hatefully. David could have even "rightfully" overthrown Saul. Meanwhile, Saul pursued David's destruction out of Saul's own insecurity (1 Samuel 18:12-16).

While God did not anoint us as parents the way He did David as king, we saw similarity in the tense relationship of authority. Jack and Ariel's parents acted defensive, insecure, and even hateful to us despite our kindness to them, just like King Saul. As foster parents, we felt we could have influenced the decision to cut off the parents' rights by laying out the ongoing facts for the judge to see. However, we believe God asked us to honor them, even though doing so was difficult when their behavior hurt us all.

Jenn

I responded to the case manager's request by writing, "You can be certain the children will always have a family in us. Check your inbox for the paperwork, but know we remain devoted to this family's restoration. We appreciate your keeping our willingness to adopt the children private from the birth parents, so they do not think we are trying to take their children from them. We don't need more drama."

Sharing these details may seem like common sense, but in foster parenting when the day-to-day care of the children becomes normal, it's tempting to start becoming the protectors of the kids living in your home. As foster parents, we dealt with the ongoing hurts the birth parents inflicted and developed strong attachments to the children. So it's tempting to fight to keep the children, like a mama cat hissing at anyone threatening her kittens. Children certainly need advocates ensuring their best interest is considered, but birth families also need to trust the motives of the people caring for their children.

Ariel continued to pray to go back to her parents by the new date circled on her calendar. By this point, the court had already extended the parents' timeline twice, so it was unlikely the judge would continue granting extensions. The parents were homeless, with no financial stability, and just a few weeks remained before the final court date. The odds did not look good.

———————————————— *Takeaways* ————————————————

If you've ever broken a glass, you know cleaning it up presents an inherent risk of cutting yourself. But if you don't clean it up, many other people will likely hurt themselves by stepping on the shattered pieces. Engaging in family brokenness comes with risks, too.

Along with the kids, we felt disappointed by broken promises of timelines for the progress of the case. This prevented or slowed the process of reunification. *Reunification* is the term used within social work to describe children returning to their parents' household after a season in state custody. Reunification is the primary goal for foster care, and it happens in about seventy percent of cases.[32] Just like repaired glass, the families resemble broken pieces, glued back together, hopefully stronger. Policies don't necessarily take into account some glasses are shattered beyond repair.

Frequently, we found ourselves hopeful, rooting for the birth parents to succeed in accomplishing everything their case plans directed within a few short months. We often failed to appreciate some of the difficulties confronting these parents. For example, some birth parents spent time in the foster care system when they were children or had siblings spend time in state custody. Growing up in a broken family tends to normalize destructive behavior, so to repeat the cycle is more normal than not. Even a task as simple as acquiring an ID card can take months when you lack a birth certificate, mailing address, or transportation.

Birth parents are also in a vulnerable position simply because they've had the state step in and take control. Some respond aggressively or defensively while others withdraw. Most want to exercise control over any aspect of the case they can. Even though the parents do not have custody of the children, they still have a lot of influence over their children's lives. At the drop of a hat, they can change their minds about appointments, traveling, and school activities, which wreak havoc on children's emotions and foster family plans.

We found the same parents who want control over their kids' lives don't necessarily take responsibility for the things they can control. More than once, children have ridden home with me sobbing after anxiously waiting all week to see their mom or dad, only to go to the office, wait for over two hours, and turn around to go home without knowing why their parents didn't show up for a visit. This sends a strong feeling of rejection. Birth parent relations vary, so we do not want to imply we found all interactions difficult or that all birth parents are the same. We've just been cut by some shards of glass, too.

Chapter 12

Rollercoaster

"The strength of a nation derives from the integrity of the home."
— **Confucius33**

Jenn

With just two weeks until the fateful court date, where a judge would determine if Jack and Ariel's parents had squandered their chance to get the kids back, tension in our household felt at an all-time high. Ariel jammed out to music, pulling herself away at all hours. She acted rude and messier than normal.

As for the case, several game-changing events transpired just prior to the court date. The kids' legal advocate, a strong voice of skepticism about the parents moved away, and he could not speak at the hearing.

Secondly, their long-term case manager was fired and replaced with a brand new case manager, unfamiliar with many of the disappointments associated with the birth parents. She empathized with the birth parents, thought they completed a lot, and pushed for reunification as soon as they could get on their feet financially. They still needed a place to live, which is no easy task for a couple frequently homeless during the last few years.

Meanwhile, I cleaned out a house we managed as a rental property. The previous tenants recently moved and left some filth, so Ariel and her buddy helped me clean to earn some extra cash. While wiping counters, I heard a prompt in my mind: "See if Jack and Ariel's parents want to live here." I thought and prayed about the idea, which seemed insane. Ludicrous. Once we returned home, I walked out to TJ who was raking leaves in the front yard and shared the pressing thought. He stopped raking, exhaled, and said, "You think the Lord told you?"

"Yes, I think so."

"Well, give the kids' mom a call and just ask some questions. Don't promise anything yet."

I went inside and called their mom. The call itself seemed radical, because a bit over a month ago we had decided to stop direct contact with each other. She manipulated things I said to bring serious repercussions against us with the Department of Children Services. Our conversations in the past often ended up creating drama for the kids. I voluntarily participated in these calls in an effort to partner with the birth parents as the staff recommended, but when they brought troubles to everyone, I stopped.

So, I called her and nervously rattled out, "I was thinking, I have a friend…and well, I'd like to help you find a place. What are you looking for and what is your ideal rent?"

Then I strolled back out to TJ, shared the information she provided, and within two weeks the parents moved into our rental house. They expressed nervous gratitude and agreed to a lease with discounted rent.

Frankly, we had serious misgivings about this idea. They were felons who had betrayed us more than once, and they had super unstable income. They consistently lied and were responsible for the dysfunction in their children's lives that we dealt with on a daily basis.

This was a Hosea moment. Hosea is a book of the Bible in the Old Testament where God asks the prophet named Hosea to marry a known prostitute. We can see where this is going to end. Marrying a whore? Yeah, that's a peaceful future. Inviting "enemies" to live in your house? Smooth sailing. I chuckled a bit as the verse came to mind, "If we are 'out of our mind,' as some say, it is for God; if we are in our right mind, it is for you" (2 Corinthians 5:13).

Even though they now had a house, it was pretty empty. So I sent out an email to the people who were involved in the kids' lives, requesting items for the family. Within days, people provided everything they needed and more. We're talking beds, dressers, a fully-supplied kitchen, gift cards, washer, dryer, grill, linens, and towels. You name it.

Their parents cried and hugged me with thanksgiving. Truly, they did not act entitled or leery but humbly received the blessing of the Lord. Even more heartwarming, Jack and Ariel seemed glad, but not surprised—as if they had faith the community would help. It made for a wildly busy couple of weeks. I managed trips to their place with donated stuff while also having my crew to care for. Being the hands that the blessings flowed through felt energizing.

TJ

The church is remarkably powerful when it relies on God. Unfortunately, due to a military training event, I did not get the opportunity to witness the body of believers come together in response to Jenn's request for provisions. When I returned home, I saw the gifts of love people bestowed upon this family, and I felt proud of our local church. Even though many of them never met these parents, they gave unselfishly from their possessions to help a family in distress.

The church's response gave me a renewed sense of optimism for this family and their situation. They had a decent home in a good location with a fresh start on life. Jenn and I had high expectations for their future.

Jenn

Whether the parents proved ready in the eyes of the judge was still to be determined. The court date arrived. I picked up the children from school early and met their parents in the parking lot. The parents looked miserable, sick, and nervous. I asked if I could pray for them, and they nodded as if unable to speak. We circled like a group hug, and I prayed with them all as we stood outside.

We waited in the lobby, and then walked into the courtroom together. The social worker declared, "Your Honor, I would like to change the Department's stance from the submitted paperwork. No longer do I recommend terminating the parents' rights. We take the position that the parents have completed their case plan, and the children should move back in with their parents immediately." Wow. Did I just hear her right?! This is almost unheard of! Court hearings usually reschedule for a future date when paperwork changes, and, furthermore, when children have lived in care this long, they normally have a drawn out transition period. They may stay with the parents on weekends for a month before going home full time.

This family's coming back together was a miracle. Now, miracles don't always result in perfect outcomes thereafter. The family is not magically transformed into the perfect family just by living under the same roof. But God saw fit and listened to the cry of His daughter Ariel.

For months she prayed, believing that by this date she would be with her parents—despite us disbelieving adults who kept giving her reasons why it was irrational, not wanting to get her hopes up.

I pulled out my camera and took pictures of the family embracing and crying in the courtroom. The future presented many challenges. The birth parents now assumed the total financial and emotional burden of parenting. Jack and Ariel would have to change schools. The time and logistical commitments would not be easy. But the sigh of relief in the courtroom was palpable. This family arrived broken and would leave restored.

Takeaways

Just as a primary measure of success in foster care is a family "reunifying," foster care succeeds when the community unifies, too. The provision of a home, furnishings, and the professional team's counsel coming together all at once for Ariel and Jack's family is a clear example of how the church can meet the needs of the community. While a competent and caring case manager was invaluable to our foster home, the voluntary support of our local church and family met many of our ongoing needs. In the day-to-day grind of life, help in the form of supplies, childcare, advocacy, mentoring, spiritual support, business services, and tutoring proved critical.

Communities set up systems for support in various ways. Some have Facebook groups to discuss various needs or extras. Others have donation centers or attics. Logistically, the local church became the most efficient facilitator in our community. With just about every placement, when we brought up the news to our Sunday school class, people quickly jumped in and offered what they could.

Without the backing of our church and friends, our experience as foster parents would have looked dramatically different. The relentless care and stress of case details often burns out foster parents. Just like with parenting one's own children, an evening or weekend away can restore sanity, improve patience, and provide a welcome opportunity for husband and wife to reconnect. Babysitting also allows foster parents to attend important extended family events, participate in mandatory training classes, or regroup during a stressful case. Those who want to babysit foster children go through a background check process. Certifying to offer short-term care is more precious than gold. Hosting children overnight in your home is called "respite care," and most fostering agencies eagerly welcome these helpers.

Foster children also need a person to formally represent their interests in court. In addition to lawyers, the court requests advocates as community volunteers of various backgrounds unrelated to child welfare or law. All kinds of wholesome American adults volunteer to serve in the roles of Court Appointed Special Advocate (CASA) or Guardian ad Litem (GALs). These individuals interact with the different people in the child's life to ensure the child receives careful attention and is heard. In some instances, the only person appointed to speak on the actual child's interest is the CASA/GAL. Unfortunately, many foster children do not have a CASA/GAL because of a lack of volunteers.

Another way to help foster children is to spend time with them. Mentoring programs exist in about every community to connect volunteers with at-risk children. Enrolling in an established program helps volunteers gain access to children during school hours and follow the children through different placements. We had a couple children involved with Big Brothers, Big Sisters, and the children cherished the one-on-one time with another loving adult. Less formally, the local church again stands strong. Older foster children in our home often participated in the youth group, and their leaders became solid role models. Younger children had Sunday school teachers or friends' parents invite the children to special play-dates. Academic tutoring met real needs, too.

And while we're talking about support, foster care desperately needs your prayers. The foster care professionals and judges require discernment and wisdom as they make life-changing decisions for dozens of children every week. Birth parents need perseverance to rebuild their lives and their parenting skills. Children and foster parents thrive on encouragement. We still remember receiving several kind notes and emails during these stressful days.

People also met real needs through their professional expertise. Our church body contained several professions—pharmacists, electricians, landscapers, cleaning businesses, bakers, doctors, retailers, therapists, government staff, and many more. All these types of individuals reached out and served our family. The local church serves as a phenomenal place for businesses to connect their talents to families.

And all of these services are just from our perspective as foster parents! Jack and Ariel's biological parents received job training, offers of bus tickets, help from counselors or parent coaches, and many more opportunities for assistance.

Chapter 13

Crash

"Every man must decide whether he will walk in the light of creative altruism or in the darkness of destructive selfishness."
— **Martin Luther King, Jr.**[34]

TJ

Just a few months after Jack and Ariel's family moved into our rental property, in the heat of summer, I called the family and asked if I could come by to see how things were going with the family and check on the house. We didn't really interact very much, but Jenn and I hoped to cultivate a relationship with the family going forward. After a greeting at the front door, I walked into the stifling hot house.

"Whoa, it's pretty warm in here. Why don't you guys have the air conditioning on?" I asked.

The mother replied, "We shut it off to save money. That's why we have all the ceiling fans running."

"Good for them," I thought. They willingly suffered through the heat without air conditioning to save money. I was proud of them for their sacrifice, but, man, it sure felt hot.

As summer turned to fall, I called and again asked if I could stop by to check on the house. I also wanted to speak with them because rent payments had gradually ceased to exist.

Prior to their moving into the house, we asked the family what they thought they could afford, and even lowered the rent to meet their level of income when needed. Unfortunately, even with the reduced rent, the parents fell several payments behind, and we needed to work out an agreement suitable to both parties.

During this visit, I walked around the side of the house into the backyard and stared at a bare concrete slab I never really noticed before. At first, I thought it was the top of a septic tank, but quickly ruled this out because the house was connected to the city sewer system. Then it dawned on me—the entire air conditioning unit was gone. There was only a concrete slab to mark the location where the unit used to sit. When I inquired about the disappearance of the air conditioner unit, no one knew anything about it.

I quickly put the willingness to go without air conditioning and a missing air conditioner unit together. After I left, I called the police and asked them how to proceed. The police officer wanted to make a report and question me, so I met the officer back at the house.

Even with a uniformed police officer questioning them, the father denied knowing anything about the mysterious disappearance of the air conditioning unit. The officer told us home and commercial air conditioning units are sometimes stolen and sold for scrap metal. I then remembered the unit connected to copper lines which ran through the attic and into the house. So the police officer and I climbed up into the attic and found all the copper tubing missing as well.

This crime took time and access. Someone had to climb into the attic to cut the lines and figure out a way to remove the air conditioning unit from a fenced backyard. Even after confronting the father with the fact the attic tubing was gone, he refused to admit any wrongdoing.

With the police officer present, I asked the family to vacate the house. I gave them a couple days, but I was concerned they might try to strip the house's electrical wiring system or do other damage before they left. Fortunately, they left the house in relatively decent shape.

We felt disappointed and discouraged. After police uncovered some other pretty significant evidence, the father finally admitted to stealing the unit. We then faced the decision of whether to press charges or not. Knowing the family and caring deeply for the children made the choice even harder.

Ultimately, we decided to press charges against the father. We concluded this based primarily upon a desire for the kids to see that poor decisions do have consequences. To be perfectly honest, I'm not sure we really had a choice. Our insurance company paid $2,400 to install a new air conditioning unit and wanted their money back. I'm sure they would have pressed charges, even if we didn't.

The hardest part for us was recognizing this decision could result in the children's return to foster care. Thankfully, the family remained intact, though homeless for a short time. We forgave the family and continue to have a limited relationship with them.

Jenn

Naturally, the theft and unpaid rent drove a wedge in our relationship with the family. With all the momentum built up to bring this family back together, the lying, stealing, and self-destruction felt like an emotional high-speed car crash. I hated that Ariel couldn't look me in the eye and that, though her mom knew she lived with a drug addict, she wouldn't get him help.

I wished for a time machine to bring me back to the week they first moved in, not so I could do something, but more like pressing a video game reset button for them. It's like after Mario falls into lava, before you get the impending "Game Over" screen. Just give them a do-over.

Words of the past also came to mind. Last summer, their court advocate shared his concern, "While these kids' being in your home is the best thing for them, and I'm very happy with you and the placement, I just don't know how they'll adjust back to living with their biological parents. Here they eat healthy meals, sleep in spacious rooms, and enjoy lots of activities. They're like typical middle class kids now. When they go home to their parents, they will experience many of the negative effects of poverty. Before, they never knew the difference. Now they do, and I don't know how well they'll adjust."

I didn't like hearing his comment and hadn't really thought of sharing our lives with the children as inflicting future pain. We tried to provide a sense of belonging and possibility. Through our lifestyle together, we wanted them to realize their full potential and experience making and achieving goals.

However, once I observed the kids back with their parents, I respected his concerns.

When Jack arrived in our home, he laid on his bed at night smiling as he told me about the time his parents moved them into a purple house. His family lived in this home for a whole year, and he remembered simple, everyday stability like going to the library and school. At reunification, when Ariel excitedly decorated her new room in our rental home, she exclaimed how, "This will be just like the purple house!" As they transitioned home, the kids spoke graciously to their parents and continually assured them, "We don't need all that stuff. We'd rather be together."

But then the blind excitement settled. Ariel called and complained about feeling unloved, but when I asked her how so, she defined love mostly through material things: "I sleep on the floor. I'm hungry. I got nothing for my birthday." She begged for her Big Sister to take her "Anywhere I can get fresh fruit and meat," whereas she would've begged for junk food when with us. So now when she's uncomfortable in poverty, she describes that discomfort as unhappy, and for her, it translates into a lack of love.

Jack is different. When he lived with us, he expressed his loyalty to his parents by embracing what he calls "low-class living." Certain activities, like proper hygiene, wearing clothing his size rather than XXL, or working for good grades he dismissed by literally saying, "That's not for low-class living like me." After living with his parents for a few months, his hair had grown long enough to cover his face, hiding the tape keeping his broken glasses together.

Takeaways

Just as we saw God's provision in bringing the family together, we knew He provided amidst the disappointment, too, but in a different way. Jesus said, "Come to me, all you who are weary and burdened, and I will give you rest. Take my yoke upon you and learn from me, for I am gentle and humble in heart, and you will find rest for your souls. For my yoke is easy and my burden is light" (Matthew 11:28-30).

We felt weary and burdened. Our hearts ached with the parent's poor choices. We had given so much of our physical, emotional, and mental energy caring for these children, and we worried if it was all in vain. What happened to an easy and light load?

When we pressed into our limits, we understood what Jesus meant. Jesus modeled dependence upon the Father when He prayed in the

Garden of Gethsemane. Jesus sought his Father's comfort while he anguished, facing more than He could handle in His confines as a man.

Luke records that God sent an angel to comfort and strengthen Jesus. While we do not compare our trials to Jesus' sacrifice, we learned through Jesus' example to ask God for comfort or relief when we anguish. When we fixed our gaze on Jesus, He lightened our burdens or provided us with the strength to persevere.

We took a risk when we handed this family the keys to one of our most valuable assets. The act of loving and giving, knowing they had free will to betray us, provided a sort of excitement and hope. When we mucked through the mud of betrayal's consequences, and settled on forgiveness, we learned something of God's faithful character. When people act disobedient, reckless, or messy, God still loves them. And if Christians are to love as God loves, an occasional crash is bound to happen. Despite the outcome, our efforts were not in vain.

Jesus did not call anyone to lead a comfortable life. His commands go against our instincts and our preferences. In many situations, we felt "comforted by God's presence but not comfortable."[35] We hope our retelling of this mess can serve to prepare and encourage rather than let a perceived or possible difficulty prevent anyone from helping a family in need. The church must continue to love and serve those around us, even if we are hurt in the process.

Chapter 14

Baby under a Bridge

"Truly I tell you whatever you did for one of the least of these brothers and sisters of mine, you did for me."

— **Jesus in Matthew 25:40**

Jenn

Casey came into state custody when his little body tested positive for drugs at birth. Furthermore, his parents were homeless. He would have gone to live under a bridge in a tent down by the river. Ironically, once social workers took him into care, Casey was homeless, too. He stayed in the hospital because case managers could not find a home for a beautiful three-day-old baby boy.

It's not that nobody wanted him. Plenty of families would love to care for Casey. But none of those families invested the time required to become certified foster parents, and therefore eligible to care for Casey. Or, families only wanted him if they could keep him forever through adoption. I mean, I did, too. Newborn babies made available for adoption often have a list of families waiting for them. Adoptive families can wait several months for a newborn baby. But many communities lack parents willing to care for a baby they might only get to love for a few months or a year.

Casey's birth happened two weeks after Jack and Ariel moved back in with their parents. The rest of us were fresh off a sixteen-hour van trip after visiting family out of state. With the laundry room still piled high with dirty clothes from the farm, we took a call asking us to welcome Casey into our family.

After some discussion and prayer, we told the case manager to keep searching for a placement, and only call back if she couldn't find a place for Casey. TJ literally worked around eighty hours a week, and I looked forward to dealing with only one case (since they were siblings) after months of emotional chaos involving four different cases. Additionally, Jasmine, Darius, and Tamika kept my days full enough, and we secretly knew TJ would deploy for an indefinite time period in four days. Legitimate excuses—am I right, guys?

Then I cried. I couldn't rest that night, tossing and praying for the little boy. In the morning, we had a voicemail from the case manager asking us to reconsider.

TJ

Jenn's a gifted mother with a lot of love to give, but caring for four children less than five years old with a husband deployed placed more burden than I wanted on her. Her tearful calls during a past deployment came immediately to my mind when we discussed whether or not to welcome Casey into our home. I said, "Jenn, I resolved to never leave you again with five kids in the home if I could avoid it. Don't you remember the calls?"

She pointed out, "This would only be four kids." I reluctantly conceded her point, but I still did not think it was a good idea. We discussed the commitment required, and we prayed. Still not on the same page, we took some time to think it over and came back together to discuss it later in the day. My primary concern involved my pending deployment and other future obligations at work. Jenn felt very strongly she could handle the additional responsibility and wanted to head to the hospital soon. We prayed together again, and I hesitantly agreed to welcome Casey into our family. Jenn immediately grabbed the phone and called the case worker to work out the details of picking up Casey from the hospital.

Jenn

I felt like it was impossible for us to say no. The idea of a homeless baby boy, held only by nurses, tore my heart. At two o'clock that afternoon, I drove to the hospital to pick him up.

Just before I turned onto the hospital's street, I received a phone call saying they found a different placement for him. So I turned around with an empty car seat, feeling neither disappointment nor relief, and retrieved my other little ones from the babysitter. TJ and I fed, bathed, and tucked in the kids, and as we fell asleep, we praised God for finding a placement for the baby.

The next afternoon I picked up the phone—yet again—and heard an exasperated case manager stating, "The placement fell through. Can we bring him over?"

I smiled, giddy with excitement, and declared "Yes" before she could finish asking.

By the afternoon, I was filled with anticipation, awaiting the transporter, Mrs. Meyer, to show up with Casey. The other children napped, so I waited in a silent house where every minute felt like an hour. She arrived; I greeted her at the door, scribbled a quick signature, and handed her the paperwork in exchange for a bundle of blanket. After passing off a plastic bag of formula and hospital discharge papers, the lady turned around and left without a word. I shouted, "Goodbye, Mrs. Meyer!" and hurried to the first chair I could find to unveil my new bundle of joy.

The exchange was like signing for a FedEx package. The best package ever.

Peeling back the blanket revealed a beautiful face peacefully asleep. I can't remember a thing I did that afternoon beside sit there and adore all five pounds of Casey. Placing my pinky in his little palm, and counting every little flaky toe. Stretching out the scrawniest little frog legs and arms, then bundling him back up into a warm embrace. Trying to wake him up to see those eyes for the first time. I can replay those first moments in my mind so clearly. Soon after his arrival, his new brother and sisters awoke from their naps and adored him with me.

TJ and I had no chance to forewarn any friends or family. I sent a picture text to our moms, and when friends arrived in the evening for the weekly Bible study we hosted, I had the best show-and-tell of my life. The beloved Holy Spirit truly took care of the details. We had everything I needed to take in a newborn baby without a trip to the store. TJ replied dryly, "Oh, yeah, we're like a real walk-in orphanage." Casey represented the eighteenth child we welcomed into our home. At this point, TJ was twenty-nine years old, and I was twenty-five. I can't say this is how we thought we would spend our twenties. It was better than I ever imagined.

TJ

When Casey arrived, the wheels almost fell off the Menn wagon. Although Jenn enjoyed caring for a newborn, Casey's needs consumed a lot of her time and energy. Tamika barely toddled around, and she often lifted up her arms for someone to carry her. Jasmine threw tantrums daily when stressed about getting dressed, exhausted after school, or confused about visitations. Darius raced through the house like every three-year-old boy. The cases required multiple appointments a week. I felt guilty and helpless accepting the responsibility of a newborn child, knowing I was leaving a few days later.

Just as He promises to do, God helped us through this tough time. One of the ways God provided for our family was by bringing a friend named Mary to live in our home for a semester while she attended college. Simply having another adult to interact with helped Jenn maintain her sanity during my deployment, and Mary occasionally watched the kids to allow Jenn a chance to complete an errand or go for a run. Though she was not acting as a nanny, her adult presence for the kids and friendship with Jenn blessed our family.

Jenn

By the weekend, TJ walked out the door to fly into combat. I didn't know when he would be back. I wept. I do every time he goes overseas. It may be normal at this point, but every time a husband or wife heads off to war, it tears at the intimacy God designed for marriage. Plus, there's the wondering of, "Is this it? Will this be the last time I see him as he is? What's he going to miss here at home?" It takes mental energy to fend off fears and lies. We stopped the routine of my bringing him to the flight hangar to say good-bye. He just left in the dark of morning, and I would pick up our truck later in the week.

This time my attention quickly shifted to the four children clamoring for love and usually food. While I do consider myself a high-capacity person for chaos, during this season, I operated emotionally and physically at full speed. As a result, a lot of other things remained undone. And time flied. Important "To Do's" whirled through my brain as I plopped on the ground to play cars with the kids and feed Casey, next to a mound of laundry to fold with dinner an hour away. I lost contact with dear friends, my counseling practice went to the backburner, and grouting the new bathroom floor for our remodeling project occurred in the wee hours of the morning between feedings.

I never thought of taking in Casey as a mistake. He is worth every ounce of me. I recall vividly praying to God, "If Casey is going to be placed somewhere else, do it fast." As quick as the thought passed off my tongue, the Holy Spirit brought an image of hiking to mind (which I planned to do with the kids over the weekend). You don't hike to be done. You hike to enjoy the journey and the perspective it brings. "Enjoy the journey, Jenny." And so we did. We enjoyed Casey's life. Every little smile and cry.

I love him to the moon and back and gasp thinking we almost missed life with Casey. Seeing his scrawny body grow within a few months into a family-record-holder for most rolls from neck to knee brought delight beyond measure.

TJ

The deployment took me away from the family for most of the first two months of Casey's life and work trips accounted for significant portions of months three and four. I think Casey was nearly four months old before I spent a complete week with him. As I came and went, I witnessed him slowly change from malnourished to chubby. His joyful, happy demeanor lightened my mood. The contrast of high-intensity missions to a cackling baby placed life in perspective.

However, my demanding schedule from work, combined with the stress of caring for four young children, caused separation to creep into our marriage. We don't think we are unique with this issue and believe many couples face considerable challenges to their marriages related to work-family balance. Our relationship could only withstand so much stress and strain without spending some time reinforcing it through date nights, quality time, or intentional conversation. As foster parents, getting away would also remind us, "These kids are not our own."

As I recognized a tension developing between us, I decided to try to figure out how the two of us could spend a night away from the kids. Again, God provided in a big way. A young couple from a local Navigator ministry offered to come to our house and watch the kids from Friday evening until Saturday night. It was one of the most caring and thoughtful gifts anyone has ever given us. Not only did they watch the children, they also completed considerable paperwork and background screenings beforehand to satisfy the state's requirements for people to watch the foster children overnight.

We left before the kids went to bed on Friday and came back after they were asleep on Saturday. Jenn had rarely been apart from Casey since his arrival. Even though she missed the kids while we left, both of us returned refreshed. Even more importantly, it benefited our marriage and our parenting.

It's amazing the difference a little time away makes. We both came back more relaxed, with greater patience, and more kindness than when we left. It was like someone hit a "reset" button in our lives. This time also gave Jenn a fresh perspective on Casey. When we left, she viewed him in much the same way as she did when he arrived—a fragile newborn. After spending a night away, she recognized how much he had grown.

We found our rhythm as a family. Casey bonded not only with Jenn and me, but also with the other three children in the home. Even though they were not biological siblings, Casey knew Jasmine, Darius, and Tamika as sisters and brother. The kids enjoyed helping feed him and playing with him, plus they held the secret to make him laugh. Our family was busy, but stable, and the children's behavior continued to improve. Both case managers asked us to consider adopting the children, so Jenn and I became mentally invested in the idea of adopting all four. The more time passed, we began to make tentative future plans based upon this assumed reality.

Jenn

My day-to-day routine centered on parenting children. I nurtured and cared for them; I prayed for them, anticipated and met needs—we shared life. We went to playgrounds and celebrated a lost tooth, a new tooth, and tied shoes.

But occasionally in the day-to-day, something would remind me that my role in their life may come to an end soon. This caused pain. Every time. Sometimes it was just a frown, or maybe a tear or words with friends.

Other times, the idea almost paralyzed me with grief—just the knowledge that separation was coming. One such moment came with Casey. I relaxed on the carpet, leaned against Darius' bunk bed, and quietly cuddled Casey. He had just woken up from a nap happy as can be and had developed into the stage of trying to take steps as I held his fingers. So he was probably ten months old. He would walk as far as my arms reach, turn back and smile in triumph, then rush back into me for a victory hug. And repeat.

Only this time, right before he woke up, his case manager called to give me two weeks' notice. Casey was moving to a relative out of state. And so when he looked back at me, smiling at another successful walk with my arms stretched out to keep him from falling, I cried. Tears flowed like a river, and I sighed a groan with clenched face as I sobbed.

He, of course, laughed because he saw I was extra proud of him. He thought I was being silly. Oh, God's grace. That boy hugged and hugged some more. At least knowing the days together were numbered kept our priorities in order as we embraced quality play.

Casey didn't leave in two weeks. The date kept getting pushed back for various reasons. He dug into a mile-high meringue cake on his first birthday, and those assisted toddles soon became conquering climbs up onto playground mounds. He fearlessly chased dogs and Tamika in circles and woke Darius up in the mornings with happy jabbering.

TJ

Meanwhile, at a court hearing we learned Casey's parents had moved into an apartment. The transition from homelessness into an apartment represented a big step. We hoped the new accommodations and some changes to their personal financial habits would result in the parents reuniting with Casey soon. After the hearing, I lingered at the courtroom to speak with a lawyer and case manager before making my way to my car. As I left the parking lot, I noticed the parents waiting at the bus stop. I pulled over and asked if they wanted a ride back into town because the county courthouse was several miles from where they lived. They happily agreed and jumped in.

From the front seat, the Birth Mother (M) excitedly asked the Birth Father (F): "Whoa! Did you see that GameStop store we just passed?"

F: "No, why?"

M: "Maybe I can go back there and buy those Xbox games I've been wanting!"

"You have an Xbox?" I asked in disbelief.

M: "Yeah. I love my Xbox, and I have all kinds of games. I'm going to go get me some new games at that GameStop back there."

"Why don't you sell the Xbox?" I asked, slightly annoyed.

M: "Why would I do that? I love my Xbox."

"But you can sell an Xbox for quite a bit of money."

M: "Yeah, I know. It was expensive. But I have money, and I play my Xbox all the time."

I tried to reason, "But if you sold the Xbox, you could use the money to buy baby clothes or furniture and pay your bills in order to get your son back quicker."

M: "But I play my Xbox all the time. I'm not selling my Xbox. No way. Psssh, sell my Xbox, what are you thinking…"

I drove the last few blocks in quiet thought, and, as they got out, they thanked me for the ride.

I do not share this story to slander birth parents, but only to show how parents' decisions directly impacted the lives of their children and everyone else involved in the case. This particular set of decisions frustrated us because the state tried so hard to help them reunite with their child. As long as they continued to place their own enjoyment ahead of their child's needs, the case would continue.

I wish this was an isolated incident, but whether it was drugs or alcohol or romance or Xbox, we saw many parents struggle with placing their child's needs before their own. In some of the most irritating instances, parents falsified tax returns claiming the children as their dependents, even when the kids were in state custody for the entire last year. The maddening part of this was not the fact they claimed them as their dependents—the exasperating part was how quickly they filed their tax returns when other administrative tasks took them months to complete.

Several times, we waited weeks or months for parents to complete simple tasks like signing papers, or getting fingerprints. It took Casey's father took five months to provide a DNA sample for a paternity test. I wish these parents showed the same diligence in working to reunite with their children as they did in filing their income tax return.

Jenn

About a year and a half after Casey's birth, God saw fit to move him out of our lives. If you are a parent, imagine the daily memories and milestones your baby made during the first sixteen months: meeting eyes, smiling, cooing, crawling, giggling, hugging, eating new foods, taking in the world of play. If I added up all the hours I had him by my side, they may outweigh that of my husband in our marriage up to that point.

TJ

Well before we knew when Casey would leave, I planned a trip to Alaska with my uncle. Neither my uncle nor I had ever visited the state, and it was a chance for us to spend some time together to view a unique part of the United States. After the trip, I planned to stay around the farm for a week to help him catch up on all the work he missed while we rambled around the Alaskan wilderness.

As the trip neared completion in Alaska, Jenn told me the state wanted to move Casey from our home before my scheduled return. So I called the airlines and changed flights to meet Jenn and the kids at her parents' house.

Spending the weekend at Jenn's parents' worked out great. Although it is never easy to say goodbye to a foster child, we remember the weekend before Casey's departure well because we shared it with close family, and the trip represented a celebration of Casey's time with us. Jenn's parents helped watch the other children to lessen the stress and strain on us while Jenn and I played with Casey. Jenn and her parents share an incredibly close bond, so they provided great support for her during this emotionally volatile time.

Eventually, Sunday night gave way to the dawn of Monday morning. I cuddled with Casey for his final hour of sleep, and we packed the van to make the trip back home where we planned to meet Casey's case managers. It was a difficult morning and a long, quiet drive home. Jenn dreaded what the next few hours would bring.

We pulled in the driveway about thirty minutes before the case manager's scheduled time to come pick Casey up. The kids played while Jenn and I packed some of Casey's last few things. When the doorbell rang, we knew the time for Casey to leave our family had come.

Jenn

TJ had to peel him out of my arms to hand him away. And then TJ held me night after night as I bawled. Oye, my tummy wrenches just thinking about it.

And like a big hole, now we are Casey-less. Life will not be the same. I feel like I'm missing an organ. He comes up in my dreams. I kept some of his baby clothes. I hang photos of us together and pull up home videos to remember his laugh. I cry out to God often on his behalf. I can't even make it through reading this chapter without crying.

But, he is not homeless anymore. When he moved from us, he went to a foster home with his brother, and then soon after that to live with a distant relative who wanted to care for him since birth, but lived out of state. He's in a loving Christian family and home. While we are totally out of reach from watching him grow up, we trust Casey is well taken care of.

Takeaways

Casey knew love. He attended supervised birth parent visits each week where his dad and mom pampered him. He had us to care for him. He had three foster siblings who entertained his every waking moment if allowed. He visited horses and puppies. He giggled often and acted fearless.

This haven of consistent, safe days is exactly the role of foster care. The attachment we built with Casey lays a foundation for his life, even if we are separated from one another. It allows for his brain to develop, to build skills, personality, and experience life. He learned the basics of trusting relationships in a stable, safe, and loving environment. Success is not defined simply as "us together." Success is based on Casey's thriving. The separation we experienced no doubt caused trauma for him, just as it did for us. But the roots he grew while starting in a loving family will keep him from withering.

At least that's what we hope. If faith is the assurance of what's hoped for, then we hope Casey will flourish and trust that God will supply his every need. We witnessed God's grace in Casey's life and believe our Heavenly Father will continue to work in Casey's life, just as He does in all our lives, to bring us into a closer relationship with Him. We consider ourselves blessed and fortunate that God used us for a season to provide Casey with a home, mommy, and daddy. We trust God is providing whatever Casey needs now.

Chapter 15

"The Old Order of Things"

"Don't cry because it's over. Smile because it happened."
— **attributed to Dr. Seuss**[36]

TJ

Several weeks after Casey's departure we took a family trip to the beach. Tamika and Jasmine enjoyed playing in the water while Darius buried his legs in the sand. Jenn pulled out peanut butter and jelly sandwiches, and everybody gathered around to grab a bite to eat. As we finished eating, I heard my phone ring.

The unfamiliar voice on the other end of the line asked if I was "Mr. Menn." After a little bit of small talk, the lady informed me that the department had decided to move the children to a different foster home. She wanted to know when we planned to return to the house so the case worker could come pick up the children. Her words hit me like someone dropping a bowling ball on my chest. I hung up the phone in a state of shock and disbelief. We remained at the beach for a couple more hours. I made a telephone call to the kids' attorney who also knew of the situation, and although she disagreed with the decision, she could not intervene. We eventually packed up and drove back to our house. Tamika, Darius, and Jasmine had lived with us for nearly two years.

Jenn

Their removal shook my world. It felt as if the state ripped them from my arms and placed them in a detrimental, possibly harmful situation—something akin to a glimpse of hell. We disagreed with a case manager that the situation was even considered good, let alone in the children's "best interest." More than our biased perspective, this situation exemplified ideological differences in opinion of what was right and just for children.

Philosophically, I disagreed with the kids' case manager on important factors like the role of kinship care, the length of time a child should spend in foster care, and transracial adoptions. With Jasmine, Darius, and Tamika, our firmly vocalized stance fell in line with federal law, but somehow two social workers worked their way around laws through bureaucratic policies or legal loopholes. We were silenced and the kids swept up in another tornado.[37]

This sense of injustice created its own flood of emotions that compounded the grief of the children's leaving. We still wrestle with it. My voice shakes when I share their stories. Sometimes I take their picture frames down for a while, or play music to get my mind off circumstances I cannot control. It's rough. For months I struggled to choose forgiveness and think kindly of those involved when I felt as if evil had won.

Not all departures are traumatic, but we tend to remember those more vividly. I cried uncontrollably during those days. More than once TJ said, "We're not doing this anymore" because of the pain we endured and the question of whether our efforts had any value if the children returned to a risky situation. The grief gagged me.

The pain with Tamika, Darius, and Jasmine lingered for months as I struggled to not let it define my days. When foster children leave, they have not died, but the relationship will never be the same and is lost. So while I'm not trying to compare our loss to the loss a parent feels when a child dies, I felt validated by Bhavya Kaushik's words:

> *When a husband loses his wife, they call him a widower... And when somebody's parents die, they call them an orphan. But there is no name for a parent, a grieving mother, or a devastated father who have lost their child. Because the pain behind the loss is so immeasurable and unbearable, that it cannot be described in a single word.*38

Thankfully, God's Spirit in us takes over when our emotional, mental, and physical strength is gone. He kept guiding my perspective to look for His evidences of grace in the situation. I actively choose to believe in God's peace and plan for the children's lives as well as for our own.

God's strong power allows me to keep putting myself in front of what I know will feel like a train wreck. It sounds like an insane idea. When I say "yes" to participating in another intimate, time consuming, costly, loving relationship that will likely end in the same way as the last one, my self-preserving nature screams, "Are you flippin' nuts?!"

Two months after Jasmine, Darius, and Tamika were abruptly removed, I wrote the following poem.

Aimlessly searching each unknown face
None I see even perceive a trace
To tell in part alas will deepen
This gripping sense of isolation.

Then writing letters to each lost
Churning memories I won't toss.
"Here are my dreams for them," I say.
Exposed without hope, there they lay.

Monuments of life ripped out
Home's a tragedy throughout
Toys like crumbles serve to cue
Crying out, "This can't be true!"

I poured into them in my presence
Now empty I slump in their absence
Not knowing the breadth of all given
Till silence reveals that I'm barren.

Mind stops racing
Eyes now spacing
Heart raw, I groan
With a sigh, alone.

You say, "Be of good cheer:
You mourn, and I am near."
More so,
You say, "I know."

Like the poem expresses, when I feel inexpressible, complicated pain, God knows. I wrote this poem while walking with God through time in prayer and reading the Bible, searching for His comfort in the midst of despair. God encourages pouring out our emotions and doubts to Him. When we take our pain to the Lord, we position ourselves to receive His healing because His presence is powerful and brings peace. Receiving the depth of healing God offers requires trusting Him as a loving Father, and faith in His ability to use what was intended for evil to bring about good (Genesis 50:20).

TJ

I firmly believe God called Jenn and me to this ministry. Through foster care, we try to advance His kingdom by loving others. We experience enormous blessings through our involvement with foster care and enjoy many incredibly rewarding moments, but saying farewell is rarely a cheerful occasion. Each time a child leaves our home, we wonder what his or her future holds. Peace overcomes feelings of anxiety when I remember God is a devoted Father who loves each of us more than we can ever comprehend.

I wish I could say we have learned to make a child's transition easy or developed a simple three-step plan for trusting God with our most pressing desires, but we haven't. When the pain of a child's departure was still fresh, we wanted to give up, quit, and close our home. I hated seeing Jenn in such pain, and her struggle caused me to reevaluate our participation as foster parents. Reading those words may sound cold, detached, or even selfish, but it's honest.

Faith is certainly required. The writer of Hebrews says, "Now faith is being sure of what we hope for and certain of what we do not see" (Hebrews 11:1). We are sure God loves these children and certain He is sovereign in this world. He will protect them, and we cling to a verse found in Matthew 18:14: "Your Father in heaven is not willing that any of these little ones should be lost."

Jenn

Without a doubt, the most common response I hear when someone learns I am a foster parent is, "I couldn't do that; it'd be so hard to let them go."

Receiving this feedback stirs up emotions. Of course there's going to be grief. I feel grateful the person speaking recognizes that transitioning a child out of my life is hard. If the comment is made while I have children in my home or in my arms, anxiety bolts through my body for a moment as I anticipate the day that will likely come all too soon. Sometimes, my mind immediately flashes to a traumatic goodbye.

I also feel a bit discouraged when I hear, "I couldn't do that," because it implies I have some special ability to bear this pain. Or do they think I don't attach as strongly to the children as their love would? Saying "I couldn't do that" also measures only the loss. It fails to see the treasure that life with the child brings.

Of course I don't think people intend to stir up all these thoughts with their statement.

The truth is I'm no different from any other woman, and God offers grace to all who believe in Jesus Christ. I survived many hard good-byes, and I expect more to come. So I'm disheartened that others, especially Christians, fear serving others because they know it will hurt.

American culture propagates a lie that says, "If something is going to hurt, you shouldn't do it." We see this lie when couples avoid vulnerable conversations or when individuals fail to sacrifice to live within their financial means. The reasoning, "I'll do the right thing, until it hurts," is synonymous with the lie.

But Truth says significant, meaningful results often require pain and difficulty. Movies like Rocky and the Biblical story of David facing

Goliath inspire us because those men faced adversity and conquered the odds. Rocky trained hard. David faced a fearful foe. Others may reap the benefits of our hardship.

The comfortable choice is not necessarily a good guide for living a righteous, loving life. This concept is at the core of the Gospel. Jesus Christ recognized the pain of the looming cross. Not only did He suffer torture and death, but He also bore the weight of the world's sin and, therefore, willingly separated Himself from the Father. Simply the knowledge of the impending suffering caused its own intense stress. While praying in the Garden of Gethsemane, Jesus felt such deep anxiety that His sweat mixed with blood. His body was falling apart. He recognized the hardship to come, yet Jesus' actions moved forward with the plan for our redemption regardless of the pending agony.

The chance to love and serve children through foster care represents the times in my life when I most closely resonated with Christ's suffering. When Christ warned His disciples of future suffering, He said, "If anyone would come after me, he must deny himself and take up his cross daily and follow me. For whoever wants to save his life will lose it, but whoever loses his life for me will save it" (Luke 9:23-24). Caring for an abused, stranded child for a season of his or her life seems like the least I can do in light of His sacrifice for us.

In more than half of our cases, we did not know the evening prior that they would leave. I believe this is God's mercy, because the eve of loss is long and hard. Emotionally, I would rather take shock than the dread of pending separation.

From the perspective of a foster mom, when the time comes, the kids are swiftly gone, and time stands still. With every child who has left our home, the Holy Spirit brought specific, Scriptural encouragement. It came through peace in prayer, encouragement from others, words of a song, or Scriptures. He spoke to me and moved in me to answer the exact concerns and doubts I wrestled with. The awareness of His presence and the voice of God tended to my needs so completely that, if I had any doubts in Jesus Christ, they were swept away.

No matter how many times I read through this chapter to write and edit, I'm a mess of tears by now. Let me assure you, amidst my grief, that I completely believe the relationships with the children and experiencing more of God's grace through them is worth one hundred times more pain. The pain is part of a sacrifice for their betterment. These kids need to experience loving, nurturing, godly parenting. How will they know life without loving attachment? The "detaching" is a cross to bear but such a light one compared to the suffering Christ carried for me.

Just as Jesus Christ is not defined by His death but rather His resurrection, so also the pain of lost children does not define us. We are about celebrating and cultivating life. We believe our relationship to each child brought greater, fuller, thriving life.

Takeaways

If we focus on Jesus and our eternity in heaven, we can make it through hard circumstances with joy. However, if we are distracted by worldly desires, we will find ourselves feeling miserable in many circumstances. If we refuse to risk our lives to love others, we miss the potential to experience the fullness of what God has for us on earth.[39]

Beyond shaping children's lives, foster parenting shaped our marriage in some profound ways. Ministering together acts as another cord to bind our marriage. We work side by side to advance God's kingdom here on earth, and that's a really exciting endeavor to share. The natural cycle of the foster care process also resulted in many more opportunities to rejoice and grieve together than we would experience otherwise. Serving children and their families rewarded us with greater intimacy, numerous chances to pray for each other, and new perspectives of one another.

More importantly, we believe spiritual seeds were sown into the lives of every child we cared for. Mealtime and nightly bedtime prayers represent some of our favorite memories. Childlike faith is so pure, and we pray this faith develops into a deeper, personal relationship with Christ as the children mature. Finally, we cling to the hope God is protecting these children wherever they currently find themselves. If we never see one another on earth again, we hope to have a joyful reunion with them in heaven where there will be no more death or mourning or crying or pain for the old order of things has passed away (Revelation 21:4).

Chapter 16

The Children We Never Knew

"'I wish it need not have happened in my time,' said Frodo. 'So do I,' said Gandalf, 'and so do all who live to see such times. But that is not for them to decide. All we have to decide is what to do with the time that is given us.'"

— J.R.R. Tolkien[40]

Jenn

It may seem like we always said "yes" to calls to take children, but TJ and I are somewhat of a rarity in the foster care world. God has said "no" to our bearing biological children right now, so we can care for more children than the average foster parents. (And while we're on the subject, people often ask with natural curiosity, "Do you plan on having children of your own?" I haven't quite figured out the right way to answer. If I respond, "Yes," the logical follow up is "When?" and I have no idea. If I say, "We're trying," then I imagine others imagining me having sex. It's just awkward.) We didn't start fostering to fill an empty nursery, but we also recognize our decision process is easier as a result.

People tell stories about life experiences, so rarely does anyone ask about the children we did not take. When children stay with us and then go, we may hurt at the end, but we know more than their names and their reports. We know their laughs, their favorite foods, their birthmarks, and we have shared memories. When we said "no" to a case manager asking about a child, it felt like we rejected the potential for a cherished relationship. It's a different kind of hard.

When we started, we chose to leave our preferences pretty wide open—any age, any race, any special need they'd allow to a young naïve couple. We had no filter for children. This general openness resulted in many opportunities to welcome children into our home.

Case managers asked us to care for several children we said "no" to. One asked us to take an eight-month-old baby girl. Saying "yes" seemed like the wrong thing with her. I'm not sure why. Days later we said "yes" to a newborn.

And then there was a sibling group of seven. We had two foster children already and only a small car. Holy smokes, my heart started racing in anxiety just hearing her say *seven* siblings. I took the call in the grocery store and thought, "That'll take three carts every trip!"

A few hours before Casey's call, the state asked us to take two girls, one of them on a feeding tube. I knew our current situation did not allow us to meet her medical needs with three children under four already in the house.

Another time we considered a thirteen-year-old pregnant teenage girl. We really contemplated this call, although once she had the baby, the number of children in our house would exceed the policy limit. States vary in the maximum number of children allowed in any one particular home. Each state usually has a formula based upon the number of bedrooms, but often the limit is around four or six, unless they're trying to keep siblings together, and then exceptions are made.

When we say "no" to a placement, the home finder continues to search for a home. They call the list of available foster families, which in some counties is long and in others is nonexistent. If they can't find a placement that day, they move to some sort of institutionalized care, whether a small family-style professional arrangement or a larger shelter.

TJ

Sometimes, we said "no" because of the children already in our home. I know many reading this may have biological children of their own and are concerned about the change in family dynamics that may accompany foster children coming into the home. I think it is wise to consider the impact fostering will have upon one's family.

I grew up in a home where my parents welcomed foster children. I remember the excitement my brother Kaleb and I felt as we waited to meet our new brother or sister. I was ten and Kaleb was eight, so we only considered the positive aspects of having someone new in the house to play with.

My parents were concerned about the effects of their decision on the household. They asked us numerous times if we had any objections to fostering and really considered every family member's opinion. When our parents consulted us in the decision-making process, it placed a little bit of responsibility on our shoulders, and we felt like teammates whose opinions mattered.

My parents also considered gender and age in reference to Kaleb and me. We normally had male foster children, although we did have some girls live with us at different times. They preferred any children who might be in our home for a long time to be younger than my brother and I. Some short-term placements of older teenagers came, but most of the children were five or under. I think my parents used wisdom in setting initial boundaries to balance opening their home to needy children while seeking to raise their own children as well.

Baby Mikey was the first child my parents brought home. My mom drove an hour to pick him up and thought he should go to a hospital instead of our home for the night. The state's Department of Children and Family Services workers thought differently. She brought him home in the front seat, back when you could do those things, with her hand on his chest monitoring his breathing. At six months old, he weighed only eight pounds.

When Mikey arrived, he was in no condition for the welcoming party I had hoped for. Mom kept him in a bassinet next to her bed as he wheezed and struggled to breathe through the night. Early the next morning, she left and went directly to the doctor's office where Mikey received breathing treatments. He steadily grew healthier the longer he stayed with us, but he remained several months behind in his development.

Kaleb and I learned so much from having Mikey in the home. We learned how to change a diaper, make bottles, burp a young child, and we gained experience raising an infant under the direction and supervision of my parents. When the time came for Mikey to leave, I remember feeling sad because I enjoyed his presence in our family and would miss him. He now smiled and giggled at supper, and his health had improved a lot. God blessed us with baby Mikey, and I think our family grew closer together as a result.

Two young brothers, ages five and three, arrived shortly after Mikey left. Jonathan and David fit the exact mold of what Kaleb and

I imagined when we thought of foster brothers: two younger boys who wanted nothing more than to be with us. Admittedly, sometimes we grew frustrated with their constant presence, but, for the most part, we had a blast with our new brothers.

Fostering has the potential to expose children to behaviors they would not otherwise witness. These behaviors can be positive or negative. For example, Jonathan and David came from a home of physical and emotional abuse. Whenever Jonathan experienced discipline or felt anxiety, he placed his back against a wall and banged his head. Even at night, sometimes I woke up to the sound of him banging his head after a bad dream. This behavior seemed so bizarre, but once my parents explained it, I felt sympathy for him and the suffering he lived with. David, to the best of my recollection, did not exhibit many signs of abuse and became the center of attention with his big brown eyes, huge smile, and infectious laugh.

Jonathan and David left our home after a year. We had formed a strong bond with them, so our family felt the loss. They both went back to their birth parents. Even as children, Kaleb and I understood our family's loss meant Jonathan and David's family was restored.

My parents' decision to foster impacted my life in numerous ways. I'm glad they didn't just say "no" because they had us. Often, Christian families attend church together and maybe join a short-term mission team for a week-long project, but our family served alongside each other on a consistent basis. I experienced the sacrifice and saw the effort they went through to provide for other people's children.

Our shared ministry helped me recognize our family's faith in Christ was more than just words, songs, or prayers. My parents modeled a servant leader attitude for us, and, even at my young age, their decision to become foster parents helped me appreciate their willingness to serve others.

Jenn

Answering a call and essentially saying, "They're not welcome here," feels like shutting a door in a child's face. And it's strange to talk about what did not happen. We wonder about them. What ever became of these children? Did they ever find a good placement? It also brings to mind the faces of thousands of children needing homes, reminding us this void is so beyond our grasp to fill. Sometimes, I pull up the county, state, or national photo listing of foster children available for adoption, some of whom live in neighborhoods where I run my errands. And I grin when their photos disappear, assuming it means they're in a family now. Though emotional torture, scroll through their pictures and stories sometime at www.heartgalleryofamerica.org. Kids out there are writing pleas for families.

Takeaways

Caseworker calls represented decision points that changed a child's life (and ours) forever. As foster parents, we always had the choice to say "yes" or "no" to any placement. It seems crazy to reflect on the enormity of some of these calls, which seemed to occur pretty frequently.

We did not utilize a formula when determining whether to say "yes" or "no" to new children coming into the home, but we did pray. Sometimes, when all feelings pointed towards saying "yes," we decided to say "no." Other times, all signs pointed toward saying "no," and we felt compelled to say "yes." During those times, we felt especially grateful for discernment from the Holy Spirit, believing He guides our choices and desires. When we said "no," we prayed for God to provide His peace and homes for these children because they needed a family to love them while going through some incredibly difficult circumstances.

Parents are wise to consider their current child-rearing obligations before jumping into foster care or, if already certified as foster parents, before agreeing to welcome an additional child or children into the home. We have heard from many people whose decision to foster or adopt is influenced by their biological children. And, if they choose to bring in additional children, each couple has different opinions about birth order, gender, race, and other distinguishing characteristics between children.

Many foster and adoptive families testify of the amazing supporting role their established children play in helping foster children thrive. Being a foster sibling brings more opportunities for character growth than any extracurricular activity we know. Oftentimes, foster siblings can help ease the transition into unfamiliar surroundings and new routines. Foster parents can love and protect their own children while bringing other children into their loving family shelter as well.

Chapter 17

Potential

"The act of facing overwhelming odds produces greatness and beauty."
—Malcolm Gladwell in David and Goliath[41]

Jenn

About a month after Jasmine, Darius, and Tamika left our home, the army moved us out of state again. We decided to take a sabbatical from fostering. We both completed our master's degrees at Harvard University's Kennedy School of Government. Among many other things, we had the opportunity to dive into the policy side of child welfare reform. I published a counseling workbook for parents, titled *Help Me Help My Child*, and TJ prepared to teach economics.

Then, we moved to West Point, New York, where we again licensed as foster parents and continue to welcome foster children into our home. (As I edit, a one year old sits on my lap while three others are just waking up.) We've found the state agency to work phenomenally well here, and we're refreshed from our season in Boston.

Regardless of what our future holds, the sacred endeavor of foster parenting blessed us. When we moved into a new place with unfamiliar people, we realized what a core element of our past foster parenting became. The framed pictures of all our past foster children on the walls of our home serve as reminders of our memories together, to pray for these precious ones, and to stay committed to the thousands of "invisible" children in the hands of America.

We choose to foster because kids need families. Community involvement is crucial, and institutions like shelters serve children well, but they cannot replace family. Research studies conducted over many decades continuously confirm that children develop best in a loving family.[42]

Countless benefits and outcomes are strengthened when children live in good, stable families. They create a sense of belonging and hope. Parents open access to community. In doing so, foster parents can change the trajectory of quality of life for both the individuals receiving care and the surrounding community. America needs quality people in this position—people like you.

Holistic, unwavering support could make foster children our national treasures. Those who overcome "underdog" situations like foster care can become the strongest members to society in values, strategy, and leadership.[43]

When foster children grow through their conflict of uncertainty and childhood maltreatment, they develop the tenacity necessary for great leadership. We know amazing adults who, as children, grew up in foster care. They met caring members of the community who helped them navigate stormy waters, and now thrive with exemplary aptitudes.

The vigor of foster care can catalyze society. In speaking of foster children in America during an interview with National Public Radio, author Cris Beam said, "They are a meter of our social problems—not just a meter of how child welfare is failing or succeeding, they're a meter of how we are failing or succeeding as a society." A US Advisory board report on child welfare published back in 1990 stated,

"Protection of children from harm is not just an ethical duty: it is a matter of national survival."[44]

ᏆᎫ

A critical component frequently missing from families today is a father. Men play an important role in helping children realize their potential, and God calls men to be fathers to the fatherless. In the beginning of the book of Isaiah, God criticizes His people Israel and tells them to fix their ways: "Stop doing wrong. Learn to do right; seek justice. Defend the oppressed. Take up the cause of the fatherless; plead the case of the widow" (Isaiah 1:16,17).

Other passages of Scripture describe men caring for the fatherless as a high value to God. For example, Job defends his righteousness by claiming he reared the fatherless (Job 31:21). As another example, Joseph had some very real and valid concerns about Mary's pregnancy (Matthew 1). Yet, he chose to be the earthly father of the Messiah, Jesus Christ. Psalm 68:5 actually ascribes this quality to God: "A father to the fatherless, a defender of widows, is God in his holy dwelling."

In his book *Wild at Heart*, John Eldredge claims every man was once a little boy who dreamed big dreams and who wanted to be the hero.[45] Thousands of little boys and little girls are waiting for a father to come into their lives, to care for them and model Christ's love to them. These children are looking for a hero.

Challenges, obstacles, and setbacks will arise in the pursuit of foster parenting, so you should prayerfully consider these things before jumping in. Sometimes simple frustrations such as professionals who do not return phone calls can cause people to think twice and not go through training.[46] Don't take it personally, and don't quit.

Sometimes you will deal with complex behavior in a child while also interacting with spiteful adults involved. Hold steady. A lot rides on your involvement. The stakes are too high for you to back out, and society needs you.

Jenn

Engaging in foster care can also lead the culture. When the world sees Christians loving and serving vulnerable children, the love of Christ is evident not through our words, but through our actions. The rising generation within the church longs for cultural leadership—not just within the four walls of church leadership.[47] We believe God will direct those who earnestly seek Him to all sorts of endeavors, one of which is foster care.

God frequently uses unlikely characters to accomplish great tasks. He intends grand purposes for every child, even those whose circumstances appear discouraging. God also teaches repeatedly how small acts of faith reap enormous results. The story of Esther demonstrates these points.

Did you know Esther was adopted? Her cousin Mordecai raised her. The Bible specifies he did more than just care for her; he "took her as his own daughter when her father and mother died" (Esther 2:7). He found a young person in need whom he could serve in a significant way, and he did.

Too often, Christians want to make such a big difference that we spend all our time thinking about, praying for, or waiting for that big purpose—searching for significance and wanting certainty that this is where God wants us to serve. All the while, "little" chances to serve pass by. When Mordecai chose to parent Esther, "It's not like he was saving a nation."[48]

When children thrive, they go on to impact many people in the world. Mordecai had no idea the generational impact his decision would make. Esther would not have likely become the king's new bride, and even if she had, her boldness came at the strong advice of her father Mordecai. He advised Esther with conviction about how we must risk ourselves and recognize God's hand in bringing us to certain places at certain times.

Maybe Esther took Mordecai's leadership to heart because he exemplified what he advised when he chose to raise her. His initial choice to care for her seemed to have a very small societal impact, yet it ended up saving the Jewish people from annihilation. Who knows how God will use our daily acts of obedience?

If you survey how you spend your days and realize you live for yourself and your family rather than for the Kingdom of God, then how about diving into a practical, needed local area? Support foster care.

It represents more than a specific call from one or two plucked-out Bible passages on orphans. Caring for neighbors is a central response of faith in God's plan. Jesus sums up His teaching as "Love God and love others." He leaves methods broad, but He does give a couple places to focus: neighbors and the least of these.

The Lord gives many people, regardless of their faith, the grace to care for others. However, when people trust in Jesus Christ for their salvation from sin, He imparts the awesome gift of the Holy Spirit. The Holy Spirit is willing to empower our lives so much that we look back at our days and know anything we accomplished happened only by the grace of God. We can keep pouring out love, joy, peace, patience, kindness, goodness, faithfulness, gentleness, and self-control because the Holy Spirit fuels our new lives in Christ. The Spirit empowers us to live beyond ourselves again and again.

The system is not perfect, and even if every person helped others, suffering would still occur. In fact, one reason we follow Jesus Christ is His promise of an eternity of problem-free living in Heaven. He says, "In this world you will have trouble—but take heart, I have overcome the world" (John 16:33).

While you hope for Heaven, bring a tangible representation of His hope through loving others. Be a part of redeeming what's been hurt and help break the cycle of brokenness.

TJ

The Scripture and promises of God come to life when we act on them. The disciples didn't spread Jesus' Gospel message by going home and studying His parables. They left Jerusalem and went to all nations because that's what God told them to do. James asks rhetorically, "What good is it, my brothers, if a man claims to have faith but has no deeds?" (James 2:14).

My hope is this book will spur you to put your faith into action. The difficulties and joys of foster parenting deepened our faith in ways we never anticipated. Your action may include foster care, or it could mean caring for an elderly parent. It might involve serving at a homeless shelter or spending more time in established ministries through your local church. Whatever role the Spirit leads you into, I hope you will follow. I pray our story will motivate people to act out their faith and love others in their communities. May God bless you as you work to advance His kingdom.

Engage with Faith to Foster

www.FaithtoFoster.com
Twitter: @FaithtoFoster
www.Facebook.com/FaithtoFosterFamilies

We encourage families who serve as foster families to post a picture on the Facebook page, along with the sign provided onsite saying, "We are a Faith to Foster family"

Read about other foster families through a series of interviews at www.FaithtoFoster.com

Please take a minute to leave a review of Faith to Foster at your online book retailer or Goodreader.com

TJ and Jenn would be glad to consider speaking at your event. Contact them through www.faithtofoster.com

How to Start Foster Parenting

Maybe you're thinking about it.

We encourage you to take the first step today by visiting the link below where you can read about foster care in your state. Information usually helps clarify a decision.

- Go to www.AdoptUSkids.org.
- Click on "For families" tab and select "State adoption and foster care information."
- Select your state. Review agency choices and contact one to attend a local orientation. This is normally a no obligation, informational monthly meeting.

Are you itching to do more now? Training might not start right away and may take two to three months. While you wait:

- Pray. Place a notecard on the refrigerator or by the computer to remind yourself to pray for the training and to prepare you for fostering.
- Schedule a family or house meeting to talk through the decision with everyone currently in the home.
- Clear your calendar for training: arrange childcare for your children and work ahead on commitments so you will have flexibility to complete the training. Frequently, training takes place on a particular day of the week, so make sure you have this day or evening free.
- Create a budget. Save a few hundred dollars to handle initial expenses with a case. Ensure you have some financial cushion to cover increased monthly expenses.
- Start a paperwork folder. Gather copies of birth and marriage certificates, driver's licenses, and proof of insurance.
- Consider purchasing a fire extinguisher and first aid kit for your home. Draw a fire escape plan.
- Contact friends and family to ask if you can use them as references. Consolidate their contact information.
- Think through bedroom arrangements, and complete any house projects that could prevent you from accepting a placement.
- Pray some more.

About the Authors

After reading our book, you know a lot about our faith and our foster parenting journey. While those two activities shape us, so do these:

TJ is a 2005 graduate of the United States Military Academy at West Point and serves as an Aviation officer in the United States Army. He earned a Master's degree in Public Policy from the John F. Kennedy School of Government at Harvard University. He and Jenn met while they were cadets, and married in December, 2005. Jenn graduated from Trinity College of the Bible and is a certified member of the Association of Certified Biblical Counselors. She later received her Master's degree in Public Administration, also from the Kennedy School at Harvard University.

We reside at West Point, New York where TJ teaches Economics in the Social Sciences Department while Jenn counsels and cares for foster children. We also enjoy spending time on the farm, playing sports, traveling, and the arts.

Endnotes

1   John F. Kennedy, "Speech to the American people", 22 October
    1962, accessed 1 April 2015 http://www.historyplace.com/
    speeches/jfk-cuban.htm

2   Diane DePanfilis and Marsha Salus, "Child Protective Services: A
    guide for case managers," *U.S. Department of Health and Human
    Services* (2003).

3   At time of writing.

4   Albert Einstein, *Living Philosophies* (New York: Simon and
    Schuster, 1931). {http://sciphilos.info/docs_pages/docs_Einstein_
    fulltext_css.html} 6 September 2013.

5   "Fostering Court Improvement" accessed 29 August 2014 www.
    fosteringcourtimprovement.com

6   Okoro, Peter. Accessed 1 April 2015 https://www.goodreads.com/
    author/show/5402429.pedro_okoro

7   Beth Moore, *Praying God's Word* (B&H Books, 2009), 189.

8   Bill Hancock, "Changing Foster Care in America: From crisis
    to community." *Faithbridge Foster Care* (2009). Accessed 20
    September 2011 www.faithbridgefostercare.org

9   Children's Bureau. "The AFCARS Report" *Adoption and Foster Care Reporting Analysis System (AFCARS). US Department of Heath and Human Services* (2012), accessed 29 August 2014.<http://www.acf.hhs.gov/sites/default/files/cb/afcarsreport20.pdf>

10 George Eliot, *Middlemarch: A Study of Provincial Life* (William Blackwood and Sons, 1907).

11 Normally foster siblings cannot share a bed, but they had a waiver for an exception to policy.

12 Goldman, Salus, Wolcott, and Kennedy, "What factors contribute to child abuse and neglect." *A Coordinated Response to Child Abuse and Neglect: The Foundation for practice* (2003), accessed 29 August 2014 https://www.childwelfare.gov/pubs/usermanuals/foundation/foundatione.cfm .

13 Cadet Prayer, accessed 1 April 2015, www.usma.edu/chaplain/sitepages/cadet%20prayer.aspx

14 Winston Churchill, accessed 1 April 2015 www.bbcamerica.com/anglophenia/2015/04/50-churchill-quotes/

15 Children's Bureau.

16 Albert Bernstein, *The Myth of Stress* (Atria Books, 2010).

17 T.S. Eliot, Preface to *Transit of Venus: Poems* by Harry Crosby (1931).

18 Gary Smalley, *The Five Love Languages* (Northfield, 2004), 20.

19 Adapted from: Bill Gothard, *Research in Principles of Life* (Institute of Basic Youth Conflicts 1981).

20 JJ Heller, "Have mercy on me." *The Pretty and the Plain* (Tag Artist Group, 2007).

21 Beth Azar, "Foster Care Has Bleak History," *APA Monitor* (November 1995), accessed 29 August 2014 www.liftingtheveil.org/foster14

22 Thomas McDonald, Reva Allen, Alex Westerfelt, and Irving Piliavin, "What we know about the effects of foster care." *IRP*

Special Report. University of Wisconsin accessed 1 April 2015 http:// www.irp.wisc.edu/publications/focus/pdfs/foc142g.pdf

23 Daniel 6, Acts 12, Exodus 14

24 Jenn walks parents through this more specifically in *Help Me Help My Child: A Biblical Counseling Workbook for Parents.* (Kimiko House Publishing 2014); Other helpful resources include Lou Priolo, *The Heart of Anger*(Calvary Press 1998); Elyse Fitzpatrick and Jessica Thompson, *Give Them Grace* (Crossway, 2011); Keck and Kubecky, *Parenting the Hurt Child* (NavPress, 2009).

25 John Piper, *Bloodlines* (Crossway 2011), 13-14.

26 National Association of Black Social Workers, *Trans-racial Adoption Position* accessed 29 August 2014. http://c.ymcdn.com/ sites/nabsw.org/resource/collection/E1582D77-E4CD-4104-996A-D42D08F9CA7D/NABSW_Trans-Racial_Adoption_1972_ Position_%28b%29.pdf

27 U.S. House of Representative Committee on Ways and Means. "Child Welfare" *Greenbook* (2012) accessed 14 August 2014 http:// greenbook.waysandmeans.house.gov/2012-green-book/chapter-11-child-welfare

28 "Fostering Court Improvement"

29 Mother Teresa, accessed 1 April 2015 http://www.brainyquote. com/quotes/keywords/poverty.html#Us8800zowJsZsipq.99

30 Jeannette Walls, *The Glass Castle: A Memoir* (Scribner, 2006).

31 I Samuel 16:13

32 "Fostering Court Improvement"

33 Confucius. *The Analects, chapter 15*, accessed 1 April 2015 http:// classics.mit.edu/Confucius/analects.html

34 Martin Luther King Jr., *Beyond Vietnam*, accessed 14 August 2014, http://www.mlkcelebration.com/mlk-the-man/famous-quotes/

35 Rick Downs, (presented at Christ the King Presbyterian Church, Cambridge, 2 February 2014). http://www.ctkcambridge.org/sermons/

36 Dr. Seuss, accessed 1 April 2015 www.goodreads.com/author/quotes/61105.Dr_Seuss

37 *Take Me Home* by Berrick and Duerr or *Nobody's Children* by Elizabeth Bartholet both explain in more detail how states use policies to get around laws in child welfare.

38 Bhavya Kaushik, *The Other Side of the Bed* (Parlance Publishers, 2013).

39 John 14:21 speaks of God's showing Himself more fully to those who obey Him. 2 Corinthians 4:16-18 likewise speaks of the energizing experience of being a vessel for Christ.

40 J., Tolkien, *Fellowship of the Ring (Mariner books, reissue 2012)*, accessed 1 April 2015 simple.wikiquote.org/wiki/The_Fellowship_of_the_Ring

41 Malcolm Gladwell, *David and Goliath: Underdogs, Misfits, and the Art of Battling Giants* (Little, Brown and Company, 2013).

42 The National Center for Child Traumatic Stress has multiple articles at www.ntcsn.org

43 Gladwell, *David and Goliath.*

44 US Advisory board report 1990, as quoted in Elizabeth Bartholet's *Nobody's Children.*

45 John Eldredge, *Wild at Heart (*Thomas Nelson, 2001).

46 Julie Wilson, "Listening to Parents" *Harvard Working Paper* (2005), 5.

47 Dr. Tim Keller's sermon to Mars Hill available on Resurgence Leadership podcast archived May 20, 2014.

48 Esther. Sermon by Kevin Meyers. 12Stone Church. Accessed 10 August 2014. https://itunes.apple.com/podcast/12stone-church-lawrenceville/id268809140?mt=2

Morgan James
Speakers Group

www.TheMorganJamesSpeakersGroup.com

We connect Morgan James published
authors with live and online events
and audiences whom will benefit
from their expertise.

Morgan James makes all of our titles available
through the Library for All Charity Organization.

www.LibraryForAll.org

Printed in the USA
CPSIA information can be obtained
at www.ICGtesting.com
JSHW022343140824
68134JS00019B/1654